ARE SOME LANGUAGES BETTER
THAN OTHERS?

'Too many linguists are afraid to pose the question that makes up the title of this book. Like people, languages are different, and each has its own strengths and weaknesses; some are harder to figure out, and some are relatively easy. Dixon illustrates these facts in a very clear and engaging manner, using examples from a wide variety of languages from around the world, and through delightful anecdotes taken from his fifty years of experience in the field. This is a book based in linguistic reality, not linguistic theory.'

Aaron D. Rubin, *Pennsylvania State University.*

'The (in)equality of languages is certainly one of the most vexing issues in modern linguistics. This book effectively challenges some common views on language, ranging from those pertaining to feelings of western cultural superiority to the 'politically correct' convictions prevalent among traditional academic circles. The author offers a balanced and well-informed discussion of the issue and draws from a lifelong research experience with languages of all types, spoken in situations that can differ dramatically. A very refreshing approach that will keep the reader fascinated.'

Willem F. H. Adelaar, *Leiden University.*

'A veritable compendium of linguistics, a collection of concise but detailed information about the essential components of human languages. It is written in an accessible, enjoyable, and refreshingly clear style. It also brings many other important questions into focus, for example, the varying extents to which speakers of diverse tongues make use of the vast potential resources of human language.'

Lars Johanson, *Language.*

'There are few limits as to the possible readership of this book. Dixon always finds a way of presenting the text not only in an intelligible but also in an entertaining format. In this way, even the unusually complex morphosyntax of Jarawara, extensively dealt with in the book, will not prevent the non-linguist from enjoying [it]. And with the wide range of typological generalizations to be found across the chapters, the book is a goldmine for any general linguist.'

Bernd Heine, *Folia Linguistica.*

R. M. W. Dixon is Adjunct Professor and Deputy Director of the Language and Culture Research Centre at James Cook University. He has written extensively on a number of Australian and Amazonian languages, as well as on ergativity, semantics, and English grammar. His many books include *The Rise and Fall of Languages* (CUP 1997), *Basic Linguistic Theory* (OUP 2010–2), *Making New Words* (OUP 2014), and *Edible Gender, Mother-in-Law Style, and Other Grammatical Wonders* (OUP 2015). Dixon's academic biography *I am a Linguist* was published by Brill in 2011.

Are Some Languages Better than Others?

R. M. W. Dixon

Language and Culture Research Centre
James Cook University

OXFORD
UNIVERSITY PRESS

OXFORD
UNIVERSITY PRESS

Great Clarendon Street, Oxford, OX2 6DP,
United Kingdom

Oxford University Press is a department of the University of Oxford.
It furthers the University's objective of excellence in research, scholarship,
and education by publishing worldwide. Oxford is a registered trade mark of
Oxford University Press in the UK and in certain other countries

© R. M. W. Dixon 2016

First published 2016
First published in paperback 2018

Published in the United States of America by Oxford University Press
198 Madison Avenue, New York, NY 10016, United States of America

British Library Cataloguing in Publication Data
Data available

Library of Congress Cataloging in Publication Data
Data available

ISBN 978–0–19–876681–0 (Hbk.)
ISBN 978–0–19–881783–3 (Pbk.)

Contents

Preface

This volume attempts a succinct portrait of the discipline of linguistics, pared down to its essentials. I have aimed to provide a representative overall view, without entering into every complexity and exception, or into rare features which occur in just a few languages. The focus is on languages as they are today, with relatively sparse mention of how languages change.

If something can be explained, it should be explainable in everyday language, which any intelligent person can understand, although of course a degree of concentration and thoughtfulness is required. I have tried to keep the use of technical terms to a minimum. Examples are quoted from a wide range of languages; these have been chosen to be simple (although not simplified), avoiding additional complexities which are irrelevant to the point being made.

Many examples are drawn from those languages I know best, from forty years of immersion fieldwork. I began by working on Dyirbal and Yidiñ, languages from the tropical rainforest of northeast Queensland, Australia. These peoples' land and culture had been ravaged by the European invader; the last generation of fluent speakers were keen that I should document the full glory of the languages. (Their grandchildren are now attempting to learn back some of the traditional languages and cultures, from the accounts which I published.) I then worked in two vibrant languages communities. First on the Boumaa dialect of Fijian, spoken amidst rainforest on the island of Taveuni. Then, venturing into the deep jungle of southern Amazonia, I studied Jarawara, a language which boasts the most awesomely complex grammar.

Chapter 1
Setting the scene

This might appear to be a dangerous book. Riots have been fomented by denigrating another's language. From time immemorial, Europeans—with their innate sense of superiority—have simply assumed that languages spoken by other kinds of people (especially those in out-of-the-way places) were 'primitive', and this has led to fierce counter-reaction.

In point of fact, none of the several thousand languages spoken today around the globe could in any sense be regarded as 'primitive'. Each has a rich vocabulary and a grammar of considerable intricacy. All present-day languages comprise a sophisticated linguistic system, which serves many social functions.

But no two languages do things in precisely the same way. Language A may be more effective in a certain respect, and language B in some other respect. Summing these up, it may turn out one language can be shown to be slightly (never more than that) superior.

The question is surely worth posing. Various aspects of the enquiry are explored in this short volume. Reviewing them, the reader will be able to decide for themself whether some languages can be considered 'better' than others (taking care to be certain what one means by 'better').

Are Some Languages Better than Others? First Edition. R. M. W. Dixon.
© R. M. W. Dixon 2016. Published 2016 by Oxford University Press.

1.1 The role of language

Language is the most vital element in the social fabric of every human society.

Each person has physical needs: sustenance, shelter, and—in a cold climate—clothing. And mental needs: a sense of identity, of well-being, of security, of reality, and of purpose. Plus the potential for aesthetic expression. Language plays an interlocking role in many aspects of life. We can survey some of its most vital functions.

(a) Language assisting in the process of belonging

Each person values their name or designation, as an emblem of their being. Also the place to which they feel they belong, and perhaps another place where they currently reside. Great importance may be attached to membership of an ethnic group, which is often associated with a particular language. People need a regular routine of living—by day, by season, by year—with familiar sequences of activities. Words, phrases, and sentences are needed to organise and discuss these.

(b) Language enabling cooperative endeavour

When a number of people are associated in some group activity, language acts as a facilitator. They may be involved in a hunting expedition, or building a house, or taking part in a sporting event. The role of language here may not be large, but it is invariably critical.

(c) Language reflecting social organisation

When a minion addresses a boss, they should employ a respectful term of address, uttered in a deferential manner. Every kind of social interaction requires nuances of vocabulary, grammar, and tone of voice—between wife and husband, parent and child, priest and parishioner, officer and infantryman.

A number of languages have speech styles which code levels of politeness, as in Japanese and Korean. In Thai there is a special speech register for talking to members of the royal family. In the case of Dyirbal, an Australian language, a special speech style must be employed in the presence of an actual or potential mother-in-law, father-in-law, son-in-law, or daughter-in-law. This shows the same grammar and phonetics as the everyday language style, but every noun, verb, and adjective has a different form.

(d)   Language used to display emotions

Whether insulting someone, or quarrelling with them, or offering support, language is the main means of expression. It may indicate anger, pride, delight, dismay, disgust, anxiety, worry, fear, curiosity, desire, appreciation, and more.

(e)   Language used to convey information

The description of events and states—telling others what has happened or is happening—constitutes a major function of language. Related to this is setting out a plan for future activity. And providing spoken instruction on how to do something, or a written manual explaining the operation of a machine.

Compiling histories of past events, and enunciating rules and laws to regulate conduct, also come under this heading.

(f)   Language as a means for aesthetic expression

Reaching beyond the necessities of life, all of humankind delights in making up stories, and enacting dramas. Songs may be functional—an integral part of some social event or amatory tryst—or purely for enjoyment. The language which fulfils purposes (a–e) is here extended, partly just for pleasure.

(g) Language as the vehicle for scholarly thought and argumentation

Language is indispensable for constructing Aristotelian syllogisms, for expounding the tenets of Freudian psychology, for investigating a cure for cancer. Also for working out relationships through a classificatory kinship system, in which each person in a small community is related to each other person through a set of intricate algorithms.

(h) Language as the conduit for proselytisation

In a campaign to get people to join a political party, or vote in a particular way, or adopt some religion, language is the means of persuasion and exhortation.

Each language which is spoken in the world today fulfils these functions, and more besides. It achieves them through a vocabulary consisting of thousands of words plus a pretty complex grammar. There is no present-day language which could be regarded as 'primitive'. However, this cannot always have been so. It will be instructive (and also fun) to speculate about what things may have been like in the distant past.

1.2 A primitive language

Humankind (*Homo sapiens*) is considered to have evolved at least 100,000 years ago, possibly much earlier. A major feature, distinguishing us from earlier stages of development, is that humans have a language—a means of communication involving contrastive vocal sounds, put together to make words, and those then combined to form sentences.

The earliest language did not simply fill a gap. There must have been an existing system of communication and this would have been steadily adapted through the incorporation of organised speech sounds.

Bodily postures, facial gestures, movements made with hand and arm, would have played a major role in communication before the evolution of language. There may have been a developed mental empathy between people within a social group, something which would have diminished once language was available to explicitly convey wants and fears. A question, 'what is it?', could have been conveyed by raised eyebrows, an injunction not to do something by a shake of the head. There would have been imitations of animal cries. A person with acute hearing might cup hand to ear and utter *Waa*, a conventionalised copy of the sound made by a wild animal, in order to warn others that a predator was nearby.

Language would, of course, have started in a small way, perhaps with just a few score words and sentences each of no more than two words. A name for each member of the group would have served for identification, used where we would employ pronouns (these are a sophisticated linguistic device which would have evolved quite a bit later). Suppose that one person, called Na, is enquiring of another, called Di, whether—having discerned a movement in the forest nearby—Di is afraid (the word for this is *ribu*).

Na utters:	Di ribu?	'Are you afraid' (literally '(Is) Di afraid?')
Di replies:	Di ribu	'I am afraid' (literally: 'Di (is) afraid')

Na might show that the first utterance is a polar question through gesture of face or hands, or by final rising intonation (as in many present-day languages).

There could have been words for 'good' and 'hot' and 'wet' with negation being added to form their antonyms: 'bad' being just 'not good', 'cold' being 'not hot', and so on. An original gesture to show negation (perhaps a head shake) would have soon been replaced by a word. The great advantage of language is that a speaker can be understood without being seen (for example, after dark, or just round a corner).

A two-word sentence would be adequate for *Di ribu* but could be a limiting factor when there are two entities involved in some activity. Suppose that Na goes out to hunt and kill (*baga*) a game animal (all large animals are covered by the general term *bibu*). Late in the afternoon, Di hears a shout from the other side of the settlement: *Na baga!* But what does it mean? Is it Na who has done the killing? Or is it the case that Na has been killed?

As our primitive language develops (which is likely to happen rather quickly), longer sentences will come to be used. And there will be some grammatical mechanism for distinguishing between who performed an action and who suffered as a result of it. (There is discussion in section 3.4 of how this may be achieved.)

1.3   What does 'better' mean?

We could describe a language a little less primitive than the one just outlined, with a couple of hundred words and sentences involving three or four words. And then, at a later stage in time (but still tens of thousands of years in the past), one slightly more advanced, in which two simple sentences can be joined together to make a complex one, something which could be translated as 'Na climbed a tree to pick fruit'.

Each of these primitive languages is better than its predecessor. And every language spoken in the world today is better than our primitive languages. Better in what way? What does 'better' mean when comparing languages?

One language is better than another to the extent that it fulfils the primary functions of a language, as sketched in section 1.1. Modern languages fulfil functions (a–h), each in its own manner, and to a greater or lesser extent. The primitive language described in section 1.2 might have been reasonably useful for (a) a sense of belonging, (b) group cooperation, and—to a very limited extent—(d) expressing emotions, and (e) conveying information. However, each modern language is more effective for every one of these four functions. The primitive language would not have been able to deal with (c) social organisation, (f) aesthetic expression, (g) argumentation, or (h) proselytising.

If we can compare a modern-day language with a primitive one, and say which is better, we must surely be able to compare two modern-day languages. Such comparison is not a simple matter, as will be illustrated in chapter 10.

Each language has a distinct infrastructure. What is expressed through the lexicon in one language may be handled within the grammar in another. Whereas in English one says *He began to eat*, an indigenous Australian would express this in Dyirbal as *Bayi* (he) *jangga-yarra-ñu*, where suffix *-yarra-* 'begin to do' is placed between verb root *janga-* 'eat' and past tense ending *-ñu*. That is, English expresses 'begin' by a separate word and Dyirbal by a grammatical suffix.

One language achieves a certain communicative function in one way and another in a second way. The first way may be more effective than the second; or vice versa. Alternatively, the two methods may be—as far as we can tell—equally effective.

There are some folk who insist that one should never try to compare the relative worth of languages. Why not? What are they afraid of? If linguistics is to be regarded as a natural science (which is a tenet I subscribe to; see section 1.5) then evaluation must be an element in its modus operandi. The doubters say that all languages are 'equal', that each language is perfect for the role it plays in the society which uses it. But if a language is perfect, why—indeed how—could it ever change? And each language is in a process of change, all the time.

Not every scientific question has a clear-cut answer. But if a question is not posed (if, indeed, a prohibition is placed on asking it) we shall never know what the answer might be.

Before moving on to discuss the diverse ways in which languages fulfil their functions, it behoves us to deal with a perennial misconception: the role of writing.

1.4 The truth about writing

Between 1963 and 2003 I undertook extensive fieldwork on Dyirbal, Yidiñ, and other Australian languages, on the Boumaa dialect of Fijian in the South Seas, and on the Jarawara language in the Amazonian jungle of Brazil, publishing a number of substantial grammars of these languages. Hearing about these endeavours, people invariably exclaim: 'But they weren't written languages, were they?' The clear implication is that, if they had no writing system in traditional times, then they weren't proper languages at all. This is simply a delusion, and unfortunately a most common one.

As already mentioned, *Homo sapiens* has been around for at least 100,000 years, maybe much longer. Language would have started out in a primitive way but it is likely to have rapidly burgeoned and—within just a few millennia—achieved a sophistication comparable to the languages of today. Yet the first writing systems, in both west and east, were only developed about five thousand years ago. For the great majority of their history, languages were just spoken. Writing is a sort-of optional extra: extremely useful in some ways, but detrimental in others. Writing is not at all necessary for the construction of a scientific argument, or for the creation of great literature.

Amongst the most revered epics in the world are Homer's *Odyssey* and *Iliad*. These were composed orally, before the introduction of writing into Greece. Indeed, Homer's own designation for a poet was *aoidos* 'singer'. The two long poems were handed down, by word of mouth, through generation after generation, until, with the advent of writing, they were put down on parchment.

Aboriginal people of northern Australia performed lengthy 'song cycles', describing the travels, experiences, and actions of ancestral beings; these would take several days to complete. The full repertoire was taught at initiation, being handed down orally though aeons of time.

Alphabets have only been invented a handful of times. The most pervasive one started in the Middle East, a little less than two thousand years BCE, to be used for Semitic languages. This was then adapted in one direction for Greek, and in another for Arabic, and in yet another for Indian languages. The Cyrillic alphabet, used for some Slavic languages, was a development from the Greek, and so was the Roman alphabet, used for

Latin. Most modern European languages employ variants of the Roman alphabet.

As European missionaries spread out over other continents, they saw it as their responsibility to devise a writing system (invariably involving letters of the Roman alphabet) and to teach people to read—in order to be able to appreciate a translation of the Bible into their language—and also to write. Was this necessarily a good thing? As Albert Schweitzer, himself a missionary, put it: 'we proceed as if not agriculture and handcraft, but reading and writing, were the beginnings of civilisation'.

In non-literate societies, people have prodigious memories, being able to recall at will histories and laws, legends and song cycles, ways of making implements and for preparing all manner of foodstuffs. Then writing came along and natural laziness took over. 'It's all there in a book, we can look it up if we need to, don't bother your mind with all that detail!' Plato quoted Socrates as saying 'if men learn this [writing], it will produce forgetfulness in their minds; they will cease to exercise memory because they rely on that which is written, calling things to remembrance no longer from within themselves, but by means of external marks.'

G. L. Kittredge, a professor of English, wrote: 'the ability of oral tradition to transmit great masses of verse for hundreds of years is proved and admitted... To this oral literature... education is no friend... When a nation begins to read... what was once the possession of the folk as a whole, becomes the heritage of the literate only, and soon, unless it is gathered up by the antiquary, vanishes altogether.' And W. G. Archer maintained, in 1943: 'if we have to single out the factor which caused the decline of English village life, we should have to say it was literacy'.

There are many pluses and also a number of significant minuses to the adoption of writing. Note that in societies with writing, the great majority of language use is oral. One thing which is perfectly certain is that the relative worth of a language does not relate to whether it has been provided with an alphabet. Indeed, we shall see in section 2.5 how writing can impede what would be desirable change in a language.

It is interesting to note that some of the most complex grammatical systems which have been described belong to languages with no written tradition. This brings up the question as to whether a grammar which is more complex than another is to be considered better, something which will be considered in chapter 6.

1.5 The science of linguistics

Linguistics can be regarded as the general science of language, parallel to mathematics as the general science of number. Pure mathematics provides a central store-house of results and methods that are drawn on by more empirical disciplines such as quantum mechanics, psephology, bridge-building, power generation, aircraft design, and much more. In similar fashion, linguistics presents a theoretical account of the nature of human language. This can be drawn on, as required, by people engaged in language teaching, translation, dictionary making, the study of literary style, cultural anthropology, philosophy, and psychology, to name but a few.

Language is a classic instance of one part only having significance with respect to the whole. Linguistics aims at providing a theoretical body of structures and systems, dealing with the whole phenomenon of language, each part interwoven with the rest. The other disciplines which relate to language may then draw on this central store-house as they wish, and will all be working in terms of the same consistent and all-embracing linguistic theory.

There are a number of possible approaches to the study of language. That which is followed here treats linguistics as a natural science, on a par with geology, biology, physics, and chemistry. The methodology is basically inductive. Detailed descriptions of the structures of individual languages are constructed, in terms of an evolved theoretical framework. The theory sets forth a number of parameters which are employed, as appropriate, in working out the grammar of a language. A particular language may reveal some new variation on an established parameter, which leads to refinement of the theory. Each grammar is cast in terms of the theory, and the theory itself is the cumulation of grammatical patterns uncovered in those languages which have thus far been thoroughly described.

All this can be demonstrated with an example. Negation is a universal feature of language. That is, each sentence is expected to make a choice between being negative (shown by *not/n't* in English, as in *John hasn't died*) and being positive (shown by zero marking in English, as in *John has died*). Suppose that a new tribe is contacted, and a bright young linguist, Emma Jilbay, analyses the structure of its language. She finds that every statement must have one of three suffixes attached to its first word. These are *-la*, which marks a positive statement, *-na* which marks a negative one, and *-dit*, indicating that it is unknown whether or not the statement is true. Thus, with noun *Jani* 'John' and verb *kapu* 'has died', we get:

Jani-la kapu	'John has died'
Jani-na kapu	'John hasn't died'
Jani-dit kapu	'It is unclear whether John has died'

Suffixes *-la, -na,* and *-dit* form a grammatical system; one—and only one—term must be selected from the system for every statement. (One can't say just **Jani kapu.*) Emma Jilbay's work shows that a grammatical system dealing with negation does not always have two terms: 'yes' and 'no'. There can be three terms: 'yes', 'no', and an uncommitted 'don't know'. The general theory is thereby refined.

Linguistics is generally reckoned to be the second oldest science (after astronomy); its beginnings were in India, before 500 BCE, with Pāṇini's magisterial grammar of Sanskrit. Like every other science, it has four fundamental tasks: description, explanation, prediction, and evaluation. We can briefly comment on these.

(a) Description. For each language, there should be a full grammar, detailing every grammatical structure, every prefix and suffix, their meanings, and their possible combinations. Each sentence in the language should be providable with a grammatical analysis. And, by applying the rules of the grammar in an appropriate manner, new sentences—which are judged as acceptable by native speakers—can be generated.

The second component is a full lexicon (or vocabulary). Every word is provided with a statement of its grammatical status (for example, 'intransitive verb'), its central meaning, and metaphorical extensions of meaning. It is carefully distinguished from semi-synonyms and contrasted with antonyms, all this being illustrated with well-chosen examples. There is also consideration of the cultural context in which a word is typically used, and its pragmatic import.

For a little-known language, there is a third component to the description: a collection of texts. These cover a variety of speakers, spanning all age-groups and both sexes. Also a range of genres—spontaneous conversations, declarations, speeches, instructions concerning fabrication and food preparation, and stories. The latter might include legends, fables, histories, accounts of current events, and autobiographies.

(b) **Explanation.** A linguist asks why something is the way it is, especially if it seems unusual or regular. The explanation can come from within a language, or from outside it.

An explanation from within is found in German. Each noun belongs to one of three genders, shown by the form of a definite article which accompanies it: *der* for masculine, *die* for feminine, and *das* for neuter. Nouns referring to male humans take *der* and most of those referring to females take *die*; for example:

der Mann	'the man'	die Frau	'the woman'
der Junge	'the boy'	die Witwe	'the widow'

However, the word for 'girl' takes the neuter article, *das Mädchen*. Why should this be?

The answer is found by examining a process of word formation. Many nouns may take the diminutive suffix -*chen*, and a word so created always takes the neuter article. For example, the word for 'duck' is feminine but its diminutive is neuter:

die Ente	'the duck'	das Entchen	'the duckling'

Mädchen 'girl' is a diminutive, based on an old noun which is no longer in active use. Thus, like all diminutives, it is classified as neuter.

An example of cultural explanation for what appears to be a grammatical oddity comes from Dyirbal, spoken in north-east Queensland. There are here four genders, marked—as in German—by an accompanying article: human males take *bayi*, human females take *balan*, edible fruit and vegetables take *balam*, and there is also a neuter gender, marked by *bala*, which is used for most non-animates (such as 'wind' and 'stone' and 'noise'). What at first seems odd is that 'sun' is feminine, *balan garri*, while 'moon' is masculine, *bayi gagara*. The explanation lies in the belief system of Dyirbal speakers—in legend, the sun is a woman and the moon her husband. The two nouns are thus allocated to genders on the basis of this characterisation.

(c) **Prediction**. This can involve saying that if a language has a certain property then there is a high chance of it having a certain other property. Or we can say that if a language has a particular make-up then it is, over time, likely to change in a specific way.

Some languages have a large open class of adjectives, with hundreds of members. In contrast there are a fair number of languages, scattered across the world, which have a small set of adjectives; these cover a common set of meanings. If Emma Jilbay reports that in her language of study there are just ten words which have special grammatical properties enabling her to recognise them as a small class of adjectives, then we can predict that these are likely to relate to dimension ('big' and 'little', 'long' and 'short'), age ('new' and 'old'), value ('good' and 'bad'), and colour ('black', 'white' and perhaps 'red'). We know that such a small adjective class is very unlikely to include any forms referring to what have been called human propensities, such as 'rude', 'jealous', and 'clever'. Such concepts will, in such a language, be rendered by either a noun (for example, 'she has cleverness') or a verb (literally 'she clevers', meaning 'she is clever').

Sciences such as geology and chemistry deal with matter, and are enabled to make exact statements. Linguistics is concerned with social events, the behaviour of humans, and, as a consequence deals in terms of compelling tendencies, and with correlations which are strong but not unconditional. We are unlikely to be able to predict the *exact* composition of Emma Jilbay's small adjective class, but we can confidently indicate the sorts of meanings which will be there.

Some categories in a grammar are independent of each other, others may show a dependence. Consider number and gender in 3rd person pronouns. In some languages (such as Hungarian) the sex of a person referred to is not shown; there is just one 3rd singular and one 3rd plural pronoun. Then there are languages with masculine and feminine forms for both 3rd singular and 3rd plural; for example, Rumanian and Modern Greek. And a considerable number of languages have a gender distinction for *just one* of the terms in the number system {singular, plural}. In such a case, gender is *always* shown in the singular, *not* in the plural, as in Russian: singular *on* 'he', *ona* 'she', and *ono* 'it', but just *oni* 'they' in the plural.

'Singular' is what is called the 'unmarked term' in a number system. If some other parameter varies with respect to number, the theory predicts that there will be more choices in singular and fewer choices in non-singular. If, for instance, the system of case affixes (showing what is subject, object, and so on) has varying size depending on number, the prediction is that there will be most distinctions in the singular.

Once a language has been fully described, with a detailed understanding of how its components interrelate, it can be possible to predict how the structural profile is likely to change, with internal connections shifting. In English the verb shows tense, as in *live-d*. There are a number of phrasal verbs, consisting of simple verb plus preposition; for example, *live off* and *take after*. The meaning of a phrasal verb cannot be inferred from the meanings of its components; each phrasal verb has to be accorded a separate dictionary entry (see section 7.5). In the present stage of the language, tense goes on the simple verb component of a phrasal verb: *he live-d off his mother, she take-s after her father*. We can predict, as a likely change, that the phrasal verb will come to be treated as a single item, with tense added to the end of it: *he live-off-ed his mother, she take-after-s her father*.

(d) **Evaluation.** A metal is needed for use within a new manufacturing process. Which would be most suitable? Following a study of relative conductivity, malleability, and durability, a decision is made concerning the best metal for the purpose. What would be the best sort of stone for re-facing a crumbling cathedral? After careful assessment, a choice is made. It is also an accepted procedure to compare the value of different economic or political systems.

Comparing two things and assessing their worth is a natural practice in most disciplines, but it is something which has by-and-large been shunned in linguistics. If linguistics is to be recognised as a science, which is my contention, it has to seriously engage in evaluation.

Just recently there has been healthy debate about the relative complexity of languages. It is accepted that one language can be more complex than another in a particular area of grammar. For instance, Dyirbal has a more complex system of genders, with four terms, than German, with three, and this is in turn more complex than the set of just two genders in French. The question is whether one can expand on this and, by comparing complexity across every area of grammar between two languages, decide that one is overall more complex than the other? This is not an easy matter. Some would argue that complexity within a pronoun system should be weighted more highly than complexity of types of comparative constructions. Others might maintain the opposite viewpoint.

This is not an endeavour which will concern us here, except tangentially, as we focus on the quite different question of whether one language can be considered better than another with respect to fulfilling the functions outlined in section 1.1. (Peeping ahead, we shall conclude, in chapter 6, that being more complex is not necessarily being better.)

The science of linguistics expounded here must be distinguished from other approaches to the study of language, such as the 'formal theories', espoused in particular by Noam Chomsky and his followers. The 'formalists' do not undertake comprehensive, theoretically-informed descriptions of languages, then generalising inductively on the basis of these. In place of this, hypotheses are put forward concerning aspects of language, with confirmation sought by examining restricted portions of languages. Formal theories come and go, each aiming to eclipse its predecessors and current competitors. In contrast, the linguistics described in this book works with a single cumulative theory, in the way that other sciences such as chemistry and geology do.

1.6 History of 'evaluations'

It is the norm for any people to consider their ethnic group, lifestyle, and language to be optimal, with all others regarded as deficient. After a visit to Paris in 1778, Dr Samuel Johnson remarked: 'What I gained by being in France was learning to be better satisfied with my own country.' The tribe I lived amongst in the Amazon jungle is called Jarawara by neighbours, but their term for themselves is 'Ee jokana', literally 'We, the real people'. All else is unreal.

There are two sides to any society, the material and the social. What is typically compared is the most visible: material objects such as tools and implements, weapons (whether spears or guns), means of transportation, machines, sophistication of dwellings, and the like. On this parameter, Europeans rank high and indigenous Australians extremely low.

A social system is implicit, and has to be lived in to be fully appreciated. Each Australian tribe had a scheme of kinship organisation, whereby each person in the community was 'related' to every other person through a complex array of algorithms. The scheme determined all social roles: who one might marry, who would be responsible for arranging a boy's initiation, or an old person's funeral, and so on. The workings of this society were thus perfectly regulated. As a minute example of the complexity involved, a Dyirbal man might only marry someone who was his father's elder sister's child's daughter, or his mother's elder brother's child's daughter, or his mother's mother's younger brother's daughter, or his mother's father's younger sister's daughter, and so on through further applications of the algorithms. On this parameter, indigenous Australians rank high and Europeans rather low.

Language is a social phenomenon. It is thus natural that intricacy of grammatical system should correlate *not* with degree of material development, but instead with sophistication of social system. It has been found that the languages with the most demanding grammars are among those spoken by small tribal groups which are high in social but low in material elaboration. Indeed, linguistic parameters tend to reflect social ones.

We can now outline three stages in assessing the worth of languages.

Stage 1, Racist evaluation. When Europeans used their ships to traverse the world, and their guns to conquer substantial territories, they came into contact with many ethnic groups. These were inferior—to varying degrees—in material culture. On this basis they were judged to be inferior people, and their languages were assumed—without evidence—to be primitive things, with just a few hundred words and at best a smattering of grammar.

The intruders, with their blinkered view, only perceived what was on the surface. In fact, these ethnic groups typically had more finely-tuned social systems than those of the invaders, and languages which were certainly as rich, often richer. It is surely significant that Europeans typically experienced considerable difficulty in mastering the local languages, whereas the conquered people soon exhibited an easy fluency in English, French, German, Spanish, Portuguese, Dutch, or whatever.

Stage 2, Redress. So pervasive was this racist evaluation that, if one was to teach the elements of linguistics, it had to be countered at once. The first pages of textbooks and the first lectures of freshman courses emphasised, as loud as was possible, that 'no language spoken in the world today is primitive' and then 'that all languages are about equal in complexity'.

Stage 3, Scientific evaluation. I suggest that, linguists having now devoted about a hundred years to redress of the racist idea, it is time to fulfil one of our missions as a science and embark on a measured evaluation of the worth of different languages. The present book aims to be a first step in this direction.

A few colleagues have counselled me against this endeavour, warning that I will be branded a racist, presumably because in some sectors the racist approach lives on. In August 1989 I was scheduled to give a talk at the Australian National University entitled 'Are some languages better than others?', with an early version of some of the ideas in the present book. A law student from Ghana came along and literally wouldn't let me speak, haranguing about having no respect for other peoples, and that African languages were not less good than European ones. Only when he ran out of breath was I able to try to explain. He had been so subjected to the racist approach that the counter-reaction was instinctive.

Chapter 2
How languages work

Language is not some sort of algebraic-type scheme, rather it is a mirror on the world, reflecting the environment in which its speakers live, their beliefs and attitudes, and their system of social organisation.

In English we have just two demonstratives: *this* (near speaker) and *that* (away from speaker). But many small communities living in mountainous terrain elaborate on this basic distinction by including information which tells whether what is being referred to is on the same level as the speaker, or higher, or lower. For example, the demonstrative system in Hua, spoken in the mountains of Papua New Guinea, is:

	SAME LEVEL	UPHILL	DOWNHILL
'this (close to speaker)'	ma	buga	muna
'that (away from speaker)'	bira	biga	mina

If the Hua were to be re-settled onto some flat country, the 'uphill'/'downhill' demonstratives would no doubt fall out of use.

Having some sort of religious belief is common to all human groups. The nature of the belief can affect structural possibilities

23

Are Some Languages Better than Others? First Edition. R. M. W. Dixon.
© R. M. W. Dixon 2016. Published 2016 by Oxford University Press.

within a grammar. For example, an Old Order Mennonite community in Canada follows an extreme form of Christianity that subordinates self to the 'will of God'. As a consequence, it is believed that an individual should not want something for themself. In keeping with this, the dialect of Pennsylvania German spoken in this community has eliminated the use of *wotte* 'want' with an infinitival complement, as in 'I want to come.' (They just don't say such things.) Cultural attitudes restrict what may be said in the language.

The indigenous peoples of Australia have classificatory kinship systems which regulate social interaction. There is a specified group of kin from which a spouse must be selected. Marriages are generally arranged in advance, by parents or uncles. Typically, a young girl—aged perhaps 5 or 7—will be promised in marriage to a boy who is a few years older. The marriage cannot take place until the girl reaches puberty, and the boy has not only undergone the male initiation rite (which involves cicatrices being incised across the stomach) but has proved himself a good hunter and provider. Dyirbal has a verb which is apposite for use in this situation. It is *ngilbin*, whose meaning includes 'look lovingly at a promised spouse'. The girl may *ngilbin*, gaze with admiration at her promised husband as he matures into a strong and handsome youth. He, in turn, will *ngilbin*, watch lovingly as his promised wife grows to become a comely maiden, adept at assisting her mother with women's tasks.

People sometimes speak of language as if the complete import of a sentence could be apparent when it is quoted in isolation. This is never the case. Each chunk of language can be fully appreciated only in terms of the linguistic event (conversation, speech, etc.) of which it is a part, and the social context within which this occurs.

2.1 The make-up of a language

A language involves two independent but interlocking parts: grammar and lexicon. The grammar is a little like a city centre—well-traversed thoroughfares, feeding into each other, replete with signs and signals and short cuts. The lexicon is somewhat akin to a parking lot—full of vehicles which will leave as needed, to engage in traffic within the city.

The lexicon (or vocabulary) consists of a number of what are generally large open-ended classes of words—nouns, adjectives, verbs, and maybe a couple more—each with some hundreds or thousands of members. New items can freely be added to each lexical class. The lexicon is discussed in chapter 7.

In contrast, grammar involves small systems, such as gender, number, and tense. Each system is closed; that is, new members may not (save in exceptional circumstances) be added. The terms in a system can be exhaustively listed, each being fully defined by the exclusion of all others. In the three-term system of singular articles in German, mentioned under (b) in section 1.5, *das* 'neuter' can be specified as 'neither *der* "masculine" nor *die* "feminine"'. One term in a grammatical system is complementary to the others.

Each language has a number of obligatory grammatical systems from which a choice *must* be made if an acceptable sentence is to be produced. The inventory of obligatory systems varies between languages. This can be illustrated by showing how to say, in three languages, that a child has fallen.

In English, count nouns need to be specified as singular (with no ending added) or as plural (shown generally by orthographic -*s*, but by -*ren* on *child*). Thus:

25

(1)   The child fell

(2)   The children fell

In Dyirbal, from Australia, there is no obligatory number system: *jaja* is 'child or children' (number *can* be specified, but by optional means). What Dyirbal does have, and English lacks, is articles showing the gender of the noun: *bayi* for masculine and *balan* for feminine. Thus, with verb *bajiñu* 'fell', we get:

(3)   Bayi jaja bajiñu   'The male child or children fell'

(4)   Balan jaja bajiñu   'The female child or children fell'

The fact that languages have different obligatory grammatical systems makes for difficulties of translation. Asked to render (1) in Dyirbal, a translator would need to enquire about the sex of the child in order to decide which of (3) and (4) is appropriate. Similarly, asked to translate (3) into English, information has to be obtained about the number of children involved, to choose between (1) and (2).

Let us now see how to describe the same event in Jarawara from Amazonia.

There are in this language only four nouns which have distinct singular and plural forms; they are 'spirit', 'man', 'woman', and 'child', which is singular *inamatewe* 'child' and plural *matehe* 'children'.

To show past tense, a verb in Jarawara takes a suffix which requires choices from three grammatical systems:

- How far in the past: immediate past is used for anything which happened from a moment ago to a few months in the past, recent past extends from a few months to a few years ago, with far past reserved for an event many years back.

- Gender: is the subject of the verb feminine (f) or masculine (m)?
- Evidence: did the speaker see the child fall, marked by eyewitness evidentiality (e), or did they not see it, marked by non-eyewitness evidentiality (n)?

There are four possible translations of English sentence (1) into Jarawara (with verb *sona-* 'fall' in immediate past tense, IP):

(5)	Inamatewe sona-hara (IP.e.f)	'The female child fell and I saw it'
(6)	Inamatewe sona-hare (IP.e.m)	'The male child fell and I saw it'
(7)	Inamatewe sona-hano (IP.n.f)	'The female child fell and I didn't see it'
(8)	Inamatewe sona-hino (IP.n.m)	'The male child fell and I didn't see it'

That is, to render (1) into Jarawara a translator needs to know how far in the past the event took place, the sex of the child, and whether or not the speaker actually saw it happen.

Of course, what *must* be said in Jarawara *can* be said in English, or in Dyirbal, by adding something like 'and I saw/ didn't see it', as a sort of optional extra. The point is that Jarawara has a two-term evidentiality system, eyewitness versus non-eyewitness, and a choice *has to be made* from this system in order to use a verb in a past tense. The speaker must commit themself as to whether or not they actually saw the child fall. Languages differ as to what has to be said.

The language which our imaginary Emma Jilbay is studying was described in section 1.5. Onto the end of the first word of every statement there must be added one of: positive -*la*, negative

-*na*, and uncommitted -*dit*. Here -*dit* 'don't know' is in an obligatory system, one term from which must be chosen in order to produce an acceptable sentence. This is quite different from the periphrastic means which may be used in other languages to convey a similar meaning (such as 'I don't know whether ... ').

The grammatical apparatus of a language also includes techniques for combining clauses to create complex sentences. For example, *The child fell and broke her arm* (coordination), *John saw [that the child had fallen]* (complement clause construction), and *Mary saw the child [who had fallen]* (relative clause construction). These are briefly discussed in section 3.6.

2.2 Phonology and redundancy

The lexical and grammatical elements of a language are represented by sounds, which are articulated by the speaker and then heard, and their meanings understood, by the hearer.

For every language, a set of phonemes can be recognised. There are speech sounds which carry a meaning contrast, and their make-up varies between languages. For example, English has contrasting phonemes /r/ and /l/; substituting one for the other produces a new word, as in /lap/ and /rap/. Jarawara, however, has a single phoneme which can be pronounced as either [r] or [l]. The most usual articulation of the name for the assai palm is [fare], but if [fale] is said, then this is recognised as the same word; [r] and [l] do not contrast in this language.

Dyirbal, in contrast, goes in the opposite direction, having three contrasting phonemes where Jarawara has one and English two. These comprise a regular *l* sound, plus two kinds of *r*; one, which is written as /r/ is like the /r/ in standard British English but with the tongue tip turned back a little further, while the other, written as /rr/, is a trill, as in Scottish pronunciation of English. The three phonemes contrast in /bulu/ 'father's father', /buru/ 'elbow', and /burru/ 'rhinoceros beetle'.

Phonemes divide into vowels (V), which function as the peak of a syllable, and consonants (C), which come at the beginning and often also at the end of a syllable. The number of consonants in a language varies from less than ten to several score (found in languages from southern Africa with a goodly array of clicks), while vowel inventories range from two to several dozen (in languages with nasalisation, a contrast between long and short vowels, and so on).

All languages have syllables of structure CV. The next most common type is CVC. English has one of the most complex syllable structures, allowing up to three consonants at the beginning and also at the end, as in *splints*. In some dialects there are even a few words with four consonants at the end of a syllable, as in the CCCVCCCC word *strengthens* /streŋθnz/.

The larger the systems of consonants and vowels, the more words there can be of a given size. For a language with just 12 consonants and 3 vowels, there are 12×3 or 36 possible monosyllables of structure CV, and 3×36 or 1,296 CVCV disyllables. Compare this with a language having 45 consonants and 16 vowels; there will be 720 possible monosyllables of type CV, and 720×720 or just over half a million disyllables CVCV. The more contrasting phonemes a language has, the shorter its words can be.

We see that there may be many phonemes and lots of short words, or a small number of phonemes, requiring longer words. The ideal phonological system lies between these extremes. The most common vowel system, across languages of the world, has five members— *i, e, a, o,* and *u*—as in Latin. English has adopted the Roman alphabet from Latin but in fact has, in the standard British dialect, six short vowels (plus unstressed ə, as at the end of *China*), five long vowels, and eight diphthongs. (These are illustrated by *din, den, dan, don, put,* and *done* for the short vowels; *dean, darn, dawn, dune,* and *turn* for the long vowels; and *deign, dine, (con)done, down, coin, dear, cairn,* and *dour* for the diphthongs.)

The average set of consonants, across languages of the world, has 20 to 24 members. Larger systems include sounds which speakers of other languages find hard to pronounce—apico-dental fricatives such as voiced /ð/ in English *though* and voiceless /θ/ in *thought*, plus whole series of ejectives, clicks, pharyngeals, and so on.

To combine adequacy of communication within a speech community and ease of learnability for people outside it, the ideal is medium-sized inventories of about 5 vowels and 20 or so consonants. This will enable the language to have words of medium length.

If a language were designed for interaction between machines—with absolute efficiency—every monosyllabic word form would be used, then every disyllabic form, before entering into trisyllabics. That is, there would be no unused 'gaps'. But natural language is used for communication between humans, who are frail beings living in an imperfect world. The hearer may not be lending their full attention, the speaker may not always enunciate in a model manner, there may be extraneous noise which impedes hearing. To counter this, all languages incorporate a goodly measure of redundancy, both in grammar and in the make-up of words.

That is, there are gaps. Not every possible word form (according to the phonological structure of the language) is assigned to an actual lexical or grammatical word. Looking at English, there are only a few gaps in some CVC frames. A few paragraphs back, I tried to illustrate 19 vowels and diphthongs of English within the frame *d–n*, and encountered six gaps: for /u/ as in *put*, /əː/ as in *turn*, /oi/ as in *coin*, /iə/ as in *dear*, /eə/ as in *cairn*, and /uə/ as in *dour*. In fact, *d–n* is one of the most-filled monosyllabic frames. With *r–m*, for instance, more than half of the possibilities are not taken up.

For disyllabic frames the gaps are more extensive. As one example, there are in English just two lexemes (that is, lexical words) relating to the frame *s–l–d*; these are *solid*, /sɔlid/, and *salad*, /saləd/. Suppose that a speaker doesn't pronounce properly and says *soled* /sɔled/, in place of *solid*. We have seen that /i/ and /e/ are contrasting phonemes; witness *din* versus *den*, *bill* versus *bell*, and so on. But there is no word *soled*; encountering *soled*, a speaker will interpret it in terms of the most similar actual word, which is *solid*. The built-in redundancy allows for communication to succeed even when (as often happens) the conditions for it are impaired.

2.3 Tones

For every articulation in a language the voice has a pitch, determined by the frequency of vibration of the vocal folds in the throat. Languages exploit variation of pitch in several ways. Typically, there will be high pitch towards the end of a question, contrasting with non-high pitch in a corresponding statement.

Around half of the languages of the world go further than this, using differences of pitch, called 'tones', to distinguish the meanings of words in the same way that vowels and consonants do. The most common system of tones has two members, marked by high and low pitch. Some languages exhibit larger systems, with up to six (or even more) contrasting tones. There are 'register tones', each having a relatively flat pitch level, and 'contour tones' (as in Chinese), which involve pitch movements, such as rising, falling, falling-rising.

In some languages each word bears a tone, in others each syllable does so. For Maale, an Omotic language spoken in southern Ethiopia, each syllable is pronounced either on a high tone, shown by an acute accent, or on a low tone, shown as grave. We can compare:

hánnó 'this'   hànnó 'today'

Just as in English a different word is produced when one vowel or one consonant phoneme is replaced by another, so in Maale a new word is here created through changing high to low tone in the first syllable.

Tone contrasts can carry grammatical meaning. For instance, gender contrast can be shown just by tone in Dhaasanac, a Cushitic language from Ethiopia:

béel 'male lover'   bèel 'female lover'

In Fur, a Nilo-Saharan language from the Sudan, replacing high by low tone on the second syllable of a word may add locative specification:

púgó 'mountain'   púgò 'on the mountain'

Is it a good thing for a language to have a system of tonal contrasts? The distinguished linguist Yuen Ren Chao provided an apposite analogy to support the contention that tones are a desirable feature: 'Since every word has some pitch pattern anyway, we might as well make use of it without any extra cost in time. A Chinese word is a sort of ice-cream cone; since you have paid for the cone as well as for the ice-cream, you might as well eat it.'

Suppose that a language has 5 vowels and 20 consonants with 10,000 possible CVCV words. If to this is added a two-term system of tones applying to each word, the possibilities become 20,000. If the tone contrast applies to each syllable, the number will rise to 40,000. The average length of words would be proportionately shorter, making for easier communication.

2.4 Dividing things up

Some concepts are always dealt with by grammar; for instance, tense. Others always fall within the realm of lexicon; these include 'dog', 'mountain', 'heavy', 'jump', and 'laugh'. Then there is a sort of middle ground, concepts which are a part of the grammar in some languages, and lexical words in others.

Most verbs refer to some activity—'hit', 'arrive', 'speak'. But verbs in English such as *begin, continue*, and *finish* refer only to a phase of an activity. If someone says *John has just begun a new book*, it could be that he has begun reading a new book, or writing one, or illustrating one, or reviewing one, or binding one. John must be beginning *something*. A statement as vague as *John has just begun a new book* will only be uttered when the speaker assumes that listeners know enough of the context to realise *what* John is beginning to do with respect to the book.

It is convenient to employ the term 'primary verbs' for verbs which have a specific reference, such as *read*, *write*, *illustrate*, *review*, and *bind*. And to use the label 'secondary concepts' for items like 'begin', 'continue', and 'finish'. In languages with rather simple word structure, like English, the secondary concepts are expressed as verbs. In languages with more complex words, they may be coded through affixes to a verb. In section 1.3, the verbal suffix *-yarra-* in Dyirbal was mentioned; from verb *bangga-* 'write' is derived *bangga-yarra-* 'begin to write'. Verbal affixes in Alamblak, a language from the Sepik region of Papua New Guinea, include *-tani-* 'complete doing' and *-tɨmbhë-* 'cease doing'.

English has modal verbs such as *can*, *may*, and *must* expressing another kind of secondary concept. In Warao, from Venezuela, there is a verbal suffix *-puhu* 'can do', and its negative *-komoni* 'can't do'. From verb root *ruhu-* 'sit up' is derived *ruhu-puhu* 'can sit up', and from *haku-* 'run' we get *haku-komoni* 'can't run'.

Quite a few languages express the secondary concept 'want' through an affix to the verb. These include Manambu, another language from the Sepik region of Papua New Guinea, where one says:

Wun yi-kər   'I (*wun*) want to (*-kər*) go (*yi-*)'

In English the concept is expressed through the verb *want*. This does have an advantage: one can say *I want to go* and also *I want John to go*. For a language like Manambu, the desiderative suffix, 'wanting', and the primary verb to which it is attached (here 'go') necessarily have the same subject. To express in Manambu

'I want John to go', it is necessary to resort to a circumlocution, something like 'I say may John go'.

'Making' is another secondary concept which is expressed grammatically in some languages. For example, in Crow (a Siouan language from Montana) there is a causative suffix *-a*; from *xachíi-* 'be moving' is derived *xachíi-a* 'make be moving, set in motion'. English does have a causative suffix *-en* which may be added to some adjectives; for instance, *deep-en* 'make (it) deep, become deep'. Other adjectives simply have to use a periphrastic construction with *make* (as do verbs); for example *make (it) shallow* (there is no **shallow-en*).

Can one technique for expressing secondary concepts be judged as more suitable than the other? There is no obvious answer to this question. The method employed accords with the overall profile of the language: grammatical means in a language with a multiplicity of affixes, and lexical means (secondary verbs) otherwise. But one thing which is clear is the easy ability to say things like *I want John to go*, where the two verbs have different subjects, in a language where 'want' is a verb in its own right.

2.5 Shifters

Most words show steady reference, but in every language there is a small set of 'shifters' whose reference changes depending on who is talking to whom, and where, and when. Consider the following dialogue between John, who is standing next to a coffee table, and Mary, who is at the far end of the room:

JOHN SAYS:	I'll leave this book here
MARY RESPONDS:	I see, you'll leave that book there
DESCRIPTION:	John leaves a copy of *Zadig* on the coffee table

There are three pairs of shifters here:

- John is referred to as *I* when he is speaking and as *you* when Mary is speaking.
- The copy of *Zadig* is referred to as *this book* by John and as *that book* by Mary.
- The coffee table is referred to as *here* by John and as *there* by Mary.

John uses *this* and *here* since the book and the coffee table are near to him, while Mary uses *that* and *there* since they are not near to her.

There are three varieties of shifter: locationals, temporals, and pronouns.

(a) Locational shifters. It appears that all languages have at least two local adverbial demonstratives, 'here (near speaker)' and 'there (distant from speaker)'. Most also have corresponding nominal demonstratives: 'this' and 'that'. Some languages have a three-term system; this is either 'near speaker', 'mid-distant from speaker', and 'far from speaker', or 'near speaker', 'near addressee', and 'not near to either'.

Distances referred to are always relative. In one story which I recorded in Fijian, the mid-distance term was used for a place a couple of kilometres away and the far-distance term for a location ten kilometres away. But in another narrative, with wider geographical scope, mid-distance was employed for twenty and far-distance for sixty kilometres.

Interestingly, Fijian combines the two kinds of three-term system. One day I was inside my house and a friend outside (who could not see in) enquired of someone sitting just inside the doorway, *Roopate qore?* He was using the mid-distance form, *qore*, to now mean 'near addressee': 'Is Roopate near you?'

Demonstratives may also include information about location up from, level with, or down from the speaker, typically just with distant terms, sometimes with both distant and near, as in the paradigm from Hua given right at the beginning of this chapter. This is another kind of shifter.

(b) Temporal shifters. Most languages have words 'yesterday', 'today', and 'tomorrow', whose reference varies according to the time of the utterance:

What is *today* today becomes *yesterday* tomorrow

People sometimes say *Tomorrow never comes*, jokingly treating *tomorrow* as if it had steady reference whereas it is in fact a shifter.

There can also be temporal shifters operating within today. Dyirbal, for instance, has *gala* 'earlier on today', *jañja* 'now', and *gilu* 'later on today'.

(c) Pronoun shifters. Every language has a 1st person pronoun (referring to the speaker) and a 2nd person pronoun (referring to the addressee). Most, but not all, languages also include a 3rd person pronoun (referring to someone other than speaker and addressee). There are almost always distinct singular and plural forms, and sometimes different forms for subject function (nominative case) and object function (accusative case).

In Old English (spoken from the fifth to the twelfth century CE) the main 1st and 2nd person forms were:

	1st singular	1st plural	2nd singular	2nd plural
subject function	ic	wē	thū	yē
object function	mē	ūs	thē	ēow

The 1st person forms came through into Modern English in recognisable shape. However, significant changes have affected 2nd person. First, 2nd plural object form *you* (from *ēow*) was used also in subject function, usurping *ye*. Then the original plural pronoun, *you*, came to be used in all formal contexts and the original singular pronoun, *thou/thee*, only in informal or intimate circumstances (rather like *vous* and *tu* in French today). Then the situations deemed appropriate for the use of *thou/thee* diminished, until finally *you* was employed for all reference to (one or more) addressee(s), producing the modern pronouns:

	1st singular	1st plural	2nd singular/plural
subject function	I	we	you
object function	me	us	

This is an unusual system. In rare circumstances it may be an advantage to be vague. But, most of the time, not having a distinction between singular and plural 2nd person is a severe disadvantage. For example, if someone asks me *Can you come to dinner with us tomorrow?*, I am unsure whether the invitation is just for me or for me and my spouse.

A language will change to eliminate an undesirable feature. New 2nd plural pronouns have been created: *y'all* in some varieties of English, *yous* in others (to name but two). But these are looked down upon as 'colloquial', and avoided, by 'educated folk' who are beholden to the authority of the written word. This is an example of how writing can stymie a desirable change, which would make the language a better vehicle for communication. If there were no writing, it is highly likely that a new 2nd plural pronoun would have spread across the entire language community.

Some languages have more than two distinctions of number in their pronouns. There may be: singular, dual, and plural (here referring to more than two). In Fijian—and in quite a few other languages—there is a four-term system: singular (referring to one person), dual (to two), paucal (to a few), and plural (to more than a few). The numerical reference of paucal and plural is relative, and varies with the context. I have heard paucal used for three or four people, contrasting with plural for seven or eight. On another occasion, paucal referred to a group of around twenty people and plural to about sixty.

Having a single 1st person plural pronoun, as English does with *we*, can lead to difficulties of communication. Suppose that John emerges from the boss's office in a somewhat shocked state and encounters his colleague Tom:

JOHN: We've just been made redundant
TOM: What! Me as well?
JOHN: No, not you, just the whole of my group

Many languages have two 1st person plural pronouns, one including and the other excluding the addressee. If English had this, John would have used the exclusive form, which would have let Tom know that his job was safe.

Jarawara has 1st plural inclusive *ee* and exclusive *otaa*. Suppose a man tells a friend that he is planning a hunting expedition into the Amazonian jungle. The choice of pronoun makes it quite clear whether or not the friend is to be included. Using verb *jete* 'go hunting', auxiliary *na*, and intention suffix *-bone*, he would choose between:

otaa jete na-bone   'We (not including you) are going out hunting'
ee jete na-bone   'We (including you) are going out hunting'

Generally, a pronoun may substitute for a noun: we can say *John went*, or *He went*, or *I went*. Some languages also have 'bound pronouns'; these are essentially affixes, which typically attach to the verb. For example, the set of bound pronouns in Warekena, an Arawak language from north-west Brazil, includes:

	prefix showing subject	suffix showing object
1st singular	nu-	-na
2nd singular	pi-	-pi
3rd singular feminine	yu-	-yu
3rd singular masculine	i-	<zero>

A sentence in Warekena can consist of a single word. For example, with verb *-wepa-* 'leave:

Nu-wepa-pi   'I am leaving you'
Pi-wepa-na   'You are leaving me'
Yu-wepa-na   'She is leaving me'

Nouns can of course be added. One can say, for instance, *neyawa* ('women') *yu-wepa-na* ('she-leave-me') 'the woman is leaving me'.

There is further discussion of bound pronouns in section 3.4.

In summary, all three varieties of shifters are a considerable aid in many functions of language; recall that they were absent from our putative primitive language, in section 1.2. A language is certainly better off for having a singular/plural contrast for all persons, and for marking an inclusive/exclusive contrast in non-singular 1st person pronouns. Would it also be a good thing to have the most possible distinctions of distance in demonstratives and of number in pronouns? This brings up the question of whether the ideal language should include every grammatical category to its maximal extent, something to which we return in chapter 8.

2.6   Types of words

The lexicon divides into word classes, the major ones being noun, verb, and adjective. The central members of the noun class refer to things, of the verb class to actions, and of the adjective class to qualities.

Word classes are recognised for each language in terms of their grammatical properties within that language. It is most import-ant to recognise that the word class of a given lexeme cannot automatically be inferred from its meaning. A few examples will illustrate this.

- In English, *beauty* is a noun with an adjective derived from it, *beautiful*. In contrast *ugly* is an adjective and a noun, *ugliness*, is derived from it. These are corresponding concepts, but one is expressed through a noun root and the other through an adjective root.
- In most languages kinship terms—such as 'father' and 'daughter'—are nouns. However, in Yuman languages from California (and in a

few others) they are verbs. These words are, after all, describing a relationship between two people. What more natural than that *John is Mary's father*, in English, should be rendered as, literally, 'John fathers Mary' (a sentence of similar structure to 'John loves Mary').

- The number 'two' is an adjective in many languages but a verb in others (for instance, Jarawara).

- The idea of needing to eat is expressed through noun *hunger* in English, through verb *ēsurio* in Latin, and through adjective *ngamir* in Dyirbal. (Interestingly, English has a derived adjective, *hungry*, formed from the noun, and Latin also has an adjective, *ēsuriens*, derived from the verb.)

- In Jarawara the translation of English *good* is a verb *amosa-* 'be good'. It takes the same inflections as verbs such as 'see', 'laugh' and 'jump', having quite different grammatical behaviour from adjectives (such as 'bad', 'big', 'little', 'new', and 'old').

Someone who was actively working on a dialect of Jarawara once told me that 'good' *must* be an adjective because 'everyone knows that in every language "good" is an adjective, since it describes a state'. This person simply hadn't mastered the basic principles of linguistic analysis.

The criteria for recognising word classes vary between languages, depending on their grammatical profiles. In Latin, words can occur in any order in a sentence but they have lots of internal structure. A word is a noun if it varies for case (see section 3.4) and it is an adjective if it varies for both case and gender. In contrast, words in English occur in a fairly fixed order and take rather few affixes. Here the criterion for a word being a noun is that it can be preceded by *the* and need not be followed by anything, and for being an adjective is that it can be preceded by *the* and followed by a noun.

Once word classes have been established on the basis of internal grammatical criteria in each language, they may be identified between languages and accorded the same name. In every language, a member of the class of nouns can function as subject and object, and an adjective may always modify a noun.

There is always similarity—but never identicality—of meanings. In all languages, 'tree', 'foot', and 'moon' are nouns. 'Mother' is a noun in most languages but a verb in some. English has noun *greed* (and derived adjective *greed-y*) whereas Dyirbal has a plain adjective *marma* 'greedy'. Fijian has a verb *puku* 'be angry' where English employs noun *anger* and derived adjective *angr-y*.

Within some languages word classes are discrete and in others they are partly overlapping.

In Latin, a noun functions only as a noun, an adjective only as an adjective, and a verb only as a verb. A root of one word class can be converted into a word of another class, but only by adding an affix. From verb root *ama-* 'love' is derived participle *amāns* 'loving', which functions as an adjective, and so on.

English is rather different with many words functioning in two (or even three) word classes. A given lexeme will have primary membership of one class, and also undertake 'double duty' in another. For example, *trap* is basically a noun, as in *He caught the rat in a trap*, and does double duty as a verb in *He trapped the rat*. A small sample of the hundreds of double-duty words is:

PRIMARY MEMBERSHIP	ALSO DOES DOUBLE DUTY AS	
noun	verb	study, fish, knife
verb	noun	change, show, mention
adjective	noun	Dutch, human, original

The phenomenon of double duty can lead to ambiguity. Consider *The Dutch study changes on a daily basis*. The word *Dutch* could be adjective or noun, and both *study* and *change* could be noun or verb. There are two distinct ways of parsing this sentence, with different meanings:

EITHER   [The Dutch$_{NOUN}$] study$_{VERB}$ changes$_{NOUN}$ on a daily basis
OR   [The Dutch$_{ADJECTIVE}$ study$_{NOUN}$] changes$_{VERB}$ on a daily basis

We should note that the ambiguity here also relates to there being two suffixes with the same form, *-s*. In the second parsing, *-s* indicates 3rd person singular subject in 'present tense' on a verb, and in the first it shows plural number on a noun. (These two parsings have the same form when written, but there may be a difference of intonation when spoken.)

Alongside the many double duty words, English also has a range of affixes which derive a word of another class. For example:

from verb *investigate* is derived noun *investigat-ion*
from verb *alter* is derived noun *alter-ation*

If we now substitute *investigate/investigation* for *study*, and *alteration/alter* for *change*, in the sentences just given, there is no ambiguity at all:

[The Dutch$_{NOUN}$] investigate$_{VERB}$ alterations$_{NOUN}$ on a daily basis
[The Dutch$_{ADJECTIVE}$ investigation$_{NOUN}$] alters$_{VERB}$ on a daily basis

The moral is that it is better (insofar as it avoids ambiguity) to have explicit derivation between word classes (such as *alter* to *alter-ation*), rather than double duty. And that having the same form for two grammatical suffixes (exemplified here by *-s*) can lead to difficulties. (See also section 7.2 and feature 36 in section 10.4.)

'Double duty' is sometimes referred to as 'conversion', and sometimes as 'zero derivation'.

Having provided a very brief sketch of how languages work, we can—in the next three chapters—examine grammatical features which appear in all languages, those which are desirable but not universal, and those which are scarcely needed.

Chapter 3
What is necessary

Grammatical features which recur in all known languages are presumably necessary components of any (non-primitive) language. What is included and what is missing here may be surprising to someone mainly familiar with the languages of Western Europe.

There are a fair number of languages (Indonesian, for example) which lack a gender system, showing that this is not a necessary part of a grammar. The semantic distinctions shown by genders in languages which have them *can* be expressed in other languages, but in a roundabout way rather than being directly coded in the grammar. For example, Indonesian has several lexical words 'female' and 'male' which can optionally be added after nouns with animate reference, to indicate the sex of what is referred to.

In English the form of a verb indicates the time (relative to the moment of speaking) of the action or state referred to; for example, *I know*PRESENT.TENSE *John and I also knew*PAST.TENSE *his father*. Many languages have a tense system, like English, but there are also many which lack one. Like gender, tense is not a necessary part of a grammar. But just as languages without gender can still indicate sex, so languages without a tense system have varied means for referring to time. Cantonese, for example,

47

Are Some Languages Better than Others? First Edition. R. M. W. Dixon.
© R. M. W. Dixon 2016. Published 2016 by Oxford University Press.

includes adverbs meaning 'originally', 'now', 'next', 'from now on', and so on.

This chapter focuses on what is found in all languages and can thus be considered 'necessary'. The sections which follow deal with statements, commands, and questions (speech acts, 3.1), negation (3.2), possession (3.3), ways of telling who instigates or controls an activity (3.4), techniques for showing identification (3.5), and ways of linking clauses together for succinct communication (3.6).

Shifters were the topic of section 2.5. Each language includes personal pronouns and demonstratives. And there is always some kind of temporal shifter. Jarawara lacks a lexeme 'tomorrow' but instead has a verbal suffix -*mina* meaning 'tomorrow' or 'in the morning'.

3.1 Speech acts

Every language provides its speakers with the wherewithal for distinguishing between the three kinds of speech act. There is a grammatical label corresponding to each:

SPEECH ACT   GRAMMATICAL LABEL (system of MOOD)
statement   declarative (or indicative)
command   imperative
question   interrogative

There are two kinds of question. A **polar question** is used when the speaker has an idea of what may or may not pertain, and seeks confirmation (or disavowal) of it, as in *Did Mary feed the dog in the garden?* This is sometimes called a 'yes/no' question since 'yes' and 'no' are likely answers, in languages which have such words (and not all languages do, as will be described in the next section).

A **content question** is used when the speaker has limited knowledge of some activity or state and—seeking information to complete the picture—uses a content question word, as in *Who fed the dog in the garden?*, *What did Mary do to the dog in the garden?*, *What did Mary feed in the garden?*, and *Where did Mary feed the dog?*

There are just a few languages which have a system of verbal affixes marking the three terms of the mood system in a tidy manner. This can be illustrated for West Greenlandic (an Eskimo language). With verb root *neri-* 'eat' and 2nd person singular subject we get:

STATEMENT	Neri-vutit	'You ate'
COMMAND	Neri-git!	'(You) eat!'
POLAR QUESTION	Neri-vit?	'Did you eat?'
CONTENT QUESTION	Su-mik neri-vit?	'What did you eat?'

The suffixes code two things: the identity of the subject (here 2nd person singular) and the mood. Suffix *-vutit* is 2sg declarative, *-git* is 2sg imperative, and *-vit* is 2sg interrogative. Note that in West Greenlandic the same suffix is used for both polar and content interrogatives. For 'What did you eat?', the content question word *su* 'what' is used, with instrumental case suffix *-mik*.

Some languages which employ suffixes for all moods mark polar and content questions differently. For instance, in Jarawara we get:

POLAR QUESTION	Aba ('fish') ti-kab(a)-ini?	'Did you eat fish?'
CONTENT QUESTION	Himata ('what') ti-kaba-ri?	'What did you eat?'

The verb -*kaba*- 'eat' takes 2nd person singular subject prefix *ti-* plus suffix *-ini* for polar interrogative and *-ri* for content interrogative.

In the great majority of languages, grammatical coding for mood is less neat. The neutral mood, declarative, may receive no special marking. Polar questions sometimes differ from statements only in having final rising intonation. Imperatives typically involve a special verb form and in many languages this is the shortest form of the verb. In Latin, for instance, the 2nd person singular imperative for *īre* 'go' is just *ī*.

The most frequent imperative involves 2nd person. In some languages this is all there can be, but others range further. West Greenlandic has imperative suffixes *-git* for 2nd person singular subject, *-gitsi* for 2nd plural, and *-ta* for 1st person plural ('Let us eat!').

In Dyirbal, if someone suggests an exchange, they may use imperative with 2nd person singular subject in one clause, and with 1st singular in a conjoined clause:

Ngurri ngaja warrgiñ   wuga,
in.turn I   boomerang give
    ngurri nginda ngaygu yarra   wuga
    in.turn you(sg) for.me fishing.line give

This is, literally, 'I give (imperative) a boomerang in turn; you give (imperative) a fishing line to me in turn.' The essence of it is: 'Let us exchange my boomerang for your fishing line'. Note that in both clauses the verb *wugal* 'give' is in its shortest form, imperative *wuga*.

Imperatives may have further features. There can be a contrast between 'near' and 'distant' forms, as in Jarawara where *kaba-hi* is 'eat (it) here and now!' and *kaba-jahi* is 'eat (it) either at a later time or in some other place!' There are languages in which verbs with a stative meaning are not permitted to be used in imperatives; one just can't say 'Regret it!' Negative imperatives may have a rather different grammar from positive ones (and it could be quite alright to say: 'Don't regret it!').

Polar questions may be recognised just by an intonation tune, or by a special order of words, as in English (for example, *Has Mary fed the dog?*), or by a grammatical marker, as in West Greenlandic and Jarawara. Or by a combination of these. In Mupun, a Chadic language from Nigeria, there are a number of contrastive markers; for example, suffix *-a* is used when the speaker expects a 'yes' answer, suffix *-wo* to express astonishment (for example, 'Did she marry someone else?'), and so on.

Content questions are always recognisable through including a content question word. There may also be a grammatical marker. The intonation varies—in some languages content questions have the same intonation as polar questions, in others it is the same as declaratives (different from that for polar questions).

There are eight standard content question words:

'who'   'what'   'which'   'how many/how much'
'where'   'when'   'why'   'how'

Few languages have eight separate forms. In Abun, from Papua New Guinea, for example, 'who' is rendered by 'which person', 'where' by 'at which', 'how' by 'like which', 'when' by 'what time', and so on.

One parameter of variation concerns whether there are one or two quantitative question words. In many languages, including English, there is one item for use with countable nouns, 'how many' (as in *how many people/knives/moons*), and another for mass nouns, 'how much' (*how much mud/blood/jealousy*). In many other languages, a single word covers both senses. Russian belongs to this group, with *skoljko* translating both *how much* and *how many* from English:

'How many dollars?' Skoljko dollarov?
'How much money?' Skoljko deneg?

Suppose that you heard someone say, in English:

John has just spent a lot of money; he's bought several cars.

A follow-up question could be just *How much?* (this necessarily refers to something uncountable and must be enquiring about the sum of money) or just *How many?* (relating to something countable, and so must be asking about the number of cars). In contrast, after a similar sentence in Russian one could not just ask *Skoljko?* since this would be ambiguous between referring to money or to cars. The interrogative *skoljko* 'how much/how many' would have to be followed by 'money' or 'cars'. The two forms in English, *how many* and *how much*, allow for a more succinct discourse.

Content question words relate to lexical word classes. 'What' generally functions like a noun, 'which' like an adjective, 'who' like a pronoun in some languages and like a noun in others, 'when' like a time word, and so on. These are found in almost all languages. What, one might then ask, about a question word relating to the class of verbs? A fairly small number of languages have this. In Dyirbal, for instance, there is *wiyama-* 'do what', which functions exactly like a regular lexical verb. Compare (here -*ñu* is the past tense suffix):

Jani wiyama-ñu 'What was John doing?'
Jani miyanda-ñu 'John was laughing'

Lacking an interrogative verb, English has to say *do what*, with *what* as object of the general verb *do*.

Returning to the general discussion, we can note that there is not always a one-to-one relation between speech acts and grammatical construction types. For example, instead of a brusque imperative, *Close the window!*, a speaker may employ a kind of command strategy, using a declarative clause, *It's cold in here*, or else an interrogative one, *Don't you feel cold?*

In summary, all languages distinguish the three main speech acts—statements, commands, and questions—but they do so with different degrees of effectiveness. For example, it is barely adequate to distinguish a statement from a polar question simply by intonation. In English, one may hear *Mary's coming tomorrow* and reply *Oh, that's good*, only to be met with *That was a question, I don't know whether or not she's coming, I was asking you.* The nuance of final rising intonation—the only clue that it was a question—had been missed, leading to misunderstanding. (Of course the first speaker could have phrased it differently, asking *Is Mary coming tomorrow?*, but in this instance they didn't.)

And, as just mentioned, it is useful to have an interrogative verb 'do what?' as well as contrasting quantitative forms 'how much' and 'how many'.

3.2 Negation

All languages have a way of negating a sentence. For a few that is all there is; others have more (outlined below).

The sentence negator can be a separate word, such as *not* (reducing to *-n't*) in English. The main verb in English may be preceded by one or more auxiliaries, and *not* follows the first of these. Thus, the negative correspondent of *Mary might have been reading Zadig* is *Mary might not have been reading Zadig*. If there is no auxiliary, then *do* is added to 'carry' the *not—Mary read Zadig* is negated as *Mary did not read Zadig*.

Alternatively, the sentence negator may be an affix. In Tariana, an Arawak language from north-west Amazonia, most verbs take a bound pronominal prefix in a positive sentence. We can get the following one-word sentences (with verb root *-nu* 'come'):

Nu-nu	'I come'	Di-nu	'He comes'
Pi-nu	'You(sg) come'	Du-nu	'She comes'

The negator consists of prefix *ma-* combined with suffix *-kade*. But a verb in Tariana may take only a single prefix, As a consequence, negator *ma-* replaces bound pronominal prefixes. We get another one-word sentence:

Ma-nu-kade 'I/you/he/she do not come'

This can, of course, be disambiguated by adjoining a free pronoun; for example *Nuha ma-nu-kade* 'I do not come', *Piha ma-nu-kade* 'You do not come'.

About 1,200 kilometres south of Tariana—but still within the vast Amazonian River basin—there is Jarawara, where negation is marked by a verbal suffix (which does not usurp any other suffix). When following a declarative suffix, the negator is *-re* if the subject of the clause is feminine and *-ra* if it is masculine. For example, if one enquired whether a man, Yobeto, was strong, a negative response would be:

Yobeto kita-ka-ra   'Yobeto is not strong'

Verb *kita-* 'be strong' is followed by the masculine form of the declarative mood suffix, *-ka,* and then the masculine form of the negator, *-ra.* (There are many other suffixes which could also be included, but all are optional.) The rules for placement of the negator are complex; for example, if there are tense and mood suffixes then the negator precedes them; if there is mood but no tense, then the negator follows it, as in the example just given. (There is more in section 6.1 on the complexities of the negative suffix in Jarawara.)

Most languages have forms 'no' and 'yes' which can constitute a single-word response to a polar question. But there are a number of languages, scattered across the globe, which lack these. Jarawara is one such. The only way to answer a question such as 'Is Yobeto strong?' is through a statement—either positive, *Yobeto kita-ka* 'Yobeto is strong', or negative, *Yobeto kita-ka-ra* 'Yobeto is not strong'. That is, the negative verbal suffixes are the only means of negation in this language.

A negative imperative most often just involves using the same negator as a declarative. English is like this; for example, *Do not read Zadig!* Other languages have a special negative imperative. In Dyirbal, for example, we get, with verb *jana-* 'stand' and pronoun *nginda* 'you (singular)':

(a)   Nginda jana-ñu   'You were standing'
(b)   Nginda gulu jana-ñu   'You were not standing'

(c) (Nginda) jana!   '(You) stand!'
(d) (Nginda) galga jana-m!   'Don't (you) stand!'

In (a–b) the verb takes past tense suffix *-ñu* and in (b) the negation of a declarative clause is shown by *gulu* 'not' before the verb. For the positive imperative, (c), the verb has a zero suffix. The negative imperative, (d), combines a special negator word, *galga* 'don't' and negative imperative verb suffix *-m*.

In most—but not all—languages, subordinate clauses can be negated. Sometimes different means are employed from those for negating a main clause. In Somali, for example, all types of clause use a preverbal negative particle, and also a special negative form of the verb. The particle is *má* in a main and *aan* in a subordinate clause.

In English, all types of clause use *not/n't*; for example:

(a) Mary didn't know [that John was dead]
(b) Mary knew [that John wasn't dead]

Sentence (a), where the main clause is negated, has a straightforward translation into Jarawara. But that language does not permit negation of a complement clause. Sentence (b) could only be rendered by a circuitous paraphrase (something like 'John wasn't dead and Mary knew it').

Some languages can negate an individual word. English does this with *no*. Compare the negated sentence, (a), with the negated noun in (b):

(a) John isn't a mathematician (he's a historian)
(b) John is no mathematician (he may think he is, but in fact he's incompetent)

There are several ways in which a sentence may include two markers of negation:

- In Spanish there is an automatic rule that if a negative word follows the verb, then the general sentence negator *no* must be included before the verb. One can say *Nadie* ('no one') *vino* ('came'), but if *nadie* is placed after *vino* then *no* is needed before it: *No vino nadie* 'No one came'.
- In many varieties of English, negation is strengthened by being expressed twice, as in *I didn't go nowhere* and *I didn't see nobody*. Schoolteachers may insist that 'two negatives make a positive', so that *I didn't see nobody* means (to them) that I did see someone. But these pundits do not employ such sentences; for those that do, they indicate emphatic negation.
- There are a few languages—such as Newar from Nepal—where a double negative does create a positive statement, and is used to make a strong assertion. For example a sentence which is, literally, 'I am unable to remain without going' means 'It is absolutely essential that I go'.

In summary, negation is a critical feature of every grammar. It is useful to include means for negating a main clause, a subordinate clause, and so on. Having a special mechanism for a negative imperative is not strictly necessary, but it does reduce the risk of misunderstanding.

3.3 Possession

Every language has the means for marking possession. In some it is rudimentary: simply juxtapose two nouns—one will be understood to be the possessor and the other the possessed. Which is which depends upon the language. The possessor comes first in Angami, a Tibeto-Burman language from north India, and it comes last in Acehnese, an Austronesian language from Sumatra. For example:

ANGAMI		ACEHNESE	
mīzə̄	phì	pintò	rumoh
table	leg	door	house
'table's	leg'	'house's	door'

In each language, a plain pronoun can be in the possessor slot (there are no possessive forms of pronouns). Thus, in Angami *á* ('I') *zēù* ('friend') 'my friend', and in Acehnese *rumoh* ('house') *lôn* ('I') 'my house'.

Many languages have a special marker to show possession. Most often this is added to the possessor and is termed 'genitive'. Examples include *'s* in English and *-de* in Mandarin:

tùzi-de	ērduō	'(a) rabbit's ear'
rabbit-GENITIVE	ear	

Alternatively, the marker of possession may be added to the possessed, and is then called 'pertensive', as in Karbi, another Tibeto-Burman language from north India:

tebul	a-keng	'table's leg'
table	PERTENSIVE-leg	

In English, as in many other languages, the same marker (here *'s*) is used for all kinds of possession. These include:

OWNERSHIP	Mary's car, the surgeon's knife
KINSHIP RELATIONSHIP	Tom's mother, the boss's wife
WHOLE–PART RELATIONSHIP	Tom's ear, the cat's paw

Where English has a single mechanism, Dyirbal employs two. Genitive suffix -*ngu* marks ownership and kin ties, while for a whole–part relationship the two words are simply juxtaposed:

Jani-ngu wangal	Jani-ngu yabu	Jani mala
'John's boomerang'	'John's mother'	'John's hand'

Many languages make a distinction between what is called 'alienable possession', covering ownership, and 'inalienable possession', for whole–part relationships. For some languages, such as Dyirbal, kin is grouped with ownership; for others—including Amele from Papua New Guinea—kin goes with whole–part. There is a further variant in Lango, a Nilotic language from East Africa, where blood relationships are marked in the same way as whole–part, and relationships by marriage are marked like ownership. This is natural: having a mother is an inalienable relationship, while a spouse is alienable (they can be divorced away).

The grammar of possession can be complex. There may be different mechanisms depending on whether the possessor is a pronoun, a proper noun, a kin term, or a common noun with human, other animate, or inanimate reference. The nature of the possessive relationship may be coded—whether it is present or past, temporary or permanent, intimate (a pet dog) or distant (a herd of cattle).

Many languages include a possessive verb similar to *have* in English but a greater number lack one. For example, there is no equivalent to *have* in Finnish, Latvian, Japanese, Amele, and Lango. What often happens is that possession is shown through a copula construction (see section 3.5), something like 'The dog is John's' or 'A dog is to John'.

In summary, it is helpful to have explicit marking for possession, the genitive-type and the pertensive-type being equally appropriate. Marking types of possession—alienable/inalienable, and so on—is helpful although not strictly necessary. Direct statements of possession are assisted by including a verb 'have'.

3.4 Who is doing it to whom

A clause consists of a predicate (a slot normally filled by a verb) and a number of arguments—these are noun phrases, headed by a noun or pronoun (optionally modified by article, demonstrative, adjectives, relative clause, etc.). Clauses divide into two types, depending on the number of core arguments their verb expects:

- an intransitive clause has an intransitive verb plus one core argument, in intransitive subject function (abbreviated as 'S')
- a transitive clause has a transitive verb plus two core arguments, in transitive subject function (abbreviated as 'A') and transitive object function (abbreviated as 'O')

Both types may optionally be extended by peripheral arguments, indicating beneficiary ('for his mother'), instrument ('with an axe'), time ('in the afternoon'), place ('at the circus'), and so on.

An intransitive clause is straightforward. There is just one core argument. If told that the words involved are 'horse' and 'jump' we know that the meaning of the clause is 'horse jumps'.

But a transitive clause is more confronting. There are two core arguments, and the grammar should provide some means for telling which is in A function (the participant who initiates and/ or controls the activity) and which is in O function (the other participant, which may be affected by the activity). Suppose that a transitive clause consists of verb 'kill' plus nouns 'father' and 'tiger'. There should be some way of telling who did what to whom—whether it was father who killed the tiger or the tiger which killed father.

Languages vary in the mechanisms they employ for this task: (a) by marking functions A and O by affixes to nouns, called 'cases'; (b) by always placing words in a fixed order; (c) through bound pronouns (introduced at the end of section 2.5); or (d) simply by context.

(a) **Using cases.** In Latin, each noun (and modifying adjective, etc.) takes a case ending; these include nominative for A function, and accusative for O. Thus, with nouns *femina* 'woman' and *puella* 'girl' plus transitive verb (in perfect form), *terr-uit* 'frightened', we get:

Femina$_A$ puella-m$_O$ terr-uit 'The woman frightened the girl'
Puella$_A$ femina-m$_O$ terr-uit 'The girl frightened the woman'

For these two nouns, nominative case (A function) is shown by zero suffix, and accusative case (O function) by suffix -*m*.

An important point to note is that in Latin words may occur in almost any order in a clause. In each of the two clauses just quoted, the three words can be arranged in any of the six possible orders (for the first, *puellam femina terruit*, or *puellam terruit femina*, and so on).

What now about marking on the S argument in an intransitive clause? Since this occurs in a different clause type, it can never co-occur with A or O, and it would be uneconomical to mark it differently from both A and O. Function S can take the same case affix as A, or the same as O. These alternatives are equally valid and practical.

Latin follows the first alternative, using nominative case for A and also for S. For example, with intransitive verb (in perfect form), *ris-it* 'laughed', we get:

Femina$_S$ ris-it   'The woman laughed'

A fair number of languages—including Dyirbal—select the other alternative, marking S in the same way as O. This is called 'absolutive' case, and the case which just marks A is termed 'ergative'. The case organisation of Latin and Dyirbal can be compared (with the forms of affixes for the nouns used here):

	A (transitive subject)	S (intransitive subject)	O (transitive object)
LATIN	nominative (zero)		accusative (*-m*)
DYIRBAL	ergative (*-nggu*)	absolutive (zero)	

We can quote the Dyirbal equivalents for the transitive clauses in Latin, using nouns *yibi* 'woman' and *nayi* 'girl', plus *marrba-ñu*, past tense of verb 'frighten (as a ghost does, or a human painted to look like a ghost)':

Nayi$_O$ yibi-nggu$_A$ marrba-ñu   'The woman frightened the girl'
Yibi$_O$ nayi-nggu$_A$ marrba-ñu   'The girl frightened the woman'

The absolutive case (a zero suffix) is used for O and also for S function, as with *miyanda-ñu*, past tense of verb 'laugh':

Yibi$_S$ miyanda-ñu   'The woman laughed'

Just like in Latin, words may occur in any order in a clause, their functions being shown by case endings.

(b) By ordering of elements. Old English had a nominative-accusative system of case marking, similar to Latin, and word order was fairly free. Then case marking for core arguments was lost (except for some pronouns) and ordering came to be fixed. One can tell which argument is which from the fact that A precedes and O follows the verb—see the translations of Latin and Dyirbal sentences just given. S also precedes, giving English an AVO, SV profile.

In languages like Latin and Dyirbal, which mark A and O by cases, the ordering of clausal elements can be put to other uses. For example, the argument which is in focus may be placed at the beginning of the clause.

Dyirbal has *-ma* as a marker of polar questions, this being added to the first word of the clause. That argument which is under focus in a polar question is placed initially, and takes *-ma*. Questions can be formed from the statement *Nayi$_O$ yibi-nggu$_A$ marrba-ñu*, 'The woman frightened the girl', in two ways:

Nayi$_O$-ma yibi-nggu$_A$ marrba-ñu 'Did the woman frighten *the girl*?' ('Was the girl the one that the woman frightened?')

Yibi-nggu$_A$-ma nayi$_O$ marrba-ñu 'Did *the woman* frighten the girl' ('Was the woman the one who frightened the girl?')

In English this focusing can only be shown by stress (indicated here by italics) or through a circumlocution.

(c) By bound pronouns. In section 2.5 there was description of how a verb in Warekena takes a prefix showing the A or S argument, and a suffix for O. These bound pronoun affixes include:

	prefix showing A in a transitive and S in an intransitive clause	suffix showing O in a transitive clause
1st singular	nu-	-na
2nd singular	pi-	-pi
3rd sg feminine	yu-	-yu
3rd sg masculine	i-	<zero>

A sentence can consist of a single word—verb root with affixes for A and O, or for S; for example *Nu-wepa-pi* 'I am leaving you'.

3rd person affixes can be expanded by nouns (or noun phrases). For example:

Neyawa	enami	i-wepa-yu	'The man is leaving the woman'
woman	man	he-leave-her	

Words can occur in any order in a clause in Warekena (as in Latin and Dyirbal). In the sentence just given, we know that *enamu* 'man' is in A and *neyawa* 'woman' is in O function from the bound pronoun affixes. Note that word order can be rearranged with no difference in meaning: *Enamu neyawa i-wepa-yu* also means 'the man is leaving the woman'.

But now consider:

Neyawa wiruberu yu-wepa-yu
woman girl she-leave-her

Here the two nouns, *neyawa* 'woman' and *wiruberu* 'girl', are both feminine and relate to the same bound pronoun. One cannot tell which is A and which O. The sentence is ambiguous between 'The woman is leaving the girl' and 'The girl is leaving the woman'.

It can be seen that bound pronouns play only a limited role in distinguishing which core argument is A and which is O for a transitive clause. They fail when the two arguments could relate to the same bound pronoun. In such circumstances, a language may bring into play an additional technique. It could employ case marking—ergative for A function or accusative for O—only when ambiguity would otherwise result. Or relative ordering may become significant, showing the functions of arguments. Or there may be neither of these, with ambiguity being resolved only by context (or perhaps not at all).

(d) **By context.** There are a number of languages (in East and South-East Asia) which lack case marking and bound pronouns, and do not have a fixed order of elements in a clause in the way that English does.

How then can the two core arguments in a transitive clause be identified—the A (whose referent may initiate and/or control the activity) and the O (the other core argument, whose referent may in some circumstances be affected by the activity)?

In many instances identification is obvious from the meaning of the words involved; for instance {plan, John, party}, {wash,

Tom, shirt}, {annoy, Mary, noise}. If the words involved are {bite, man, dog}, one would generally understand the clause to mean 'dog bites man', since this is what dogs typically do to men. But one must be able to describe an unusual activity such as 'man bites dog'.

As emphasised at the beginning of chapter 2, language is not some algebraic-type scheme but rather a living organism. Each utterance is said in a certain social and textual setting, and it is this whole context of use which gives it meaning. {bite, man, dog}, referring to the man as the aggressor, is likely to be said within a situation for which this would not be a surprising event—maybe we know that the man is a bit crazy, or perhaps he was doing it for a bet. Or there could be a following utterance: 'The dog is badly hurt, better take it to the vet', which would clarify the meaning of what had been said before.

Language is a remarkable creature, adaptable in so many ways. If the grammar does not clearly indicate which argument is A and which O, then some other way will be found.

But of course it is best to have a means of identification within the grammar. And of those discussed, case marking is clearly the most effective.

3.5 Saying what is what

Transitive and intransitive clauses have verbs which refer to actions (for example 'John cut the bread') or states ('Mary enjoyed the play'). A language also needs to describe relationships. Like many others, English achieves this through copula clauses, with *be* as the verb, and two arguments, a copula subject (CS) and a copula complement (CC). For example:

RELATIONSHIP	CS	COPULA	CC
Identity	Mary	is	my sister
	That man	is	a priest
Attribution	John	is	fat

Unlike transitive and intransitive verbs, a copula does not have any reference. It simply describes a relationship, the character of the relationship being determined by the nature of the CS and CC arguments. The CS and CC slots are filled by noun phrases, just like S, A, and O slots, plus—in English—CC can be just an adjective.

Since a copula verb has no reference, why include it? A major reason is that it is a carrier for grammatical information which in transitive and intransitive clauses is coded on the verb. For example, tense in English. We can say *That man was a priest* (but he has now been defrocked) and *John was fat* (but he has now slimmed down).

A copula clause may be used for other kinds of identification, such as Possession (*This book is mine*), Benefactive (*The present is for John*), and Location (*The mower is in the shed*).

Some languages do not include a copula in their grammar, but show identification by just juxtaposing two noun phrases within a verbless clause, as in Dyirbal:

Jani jami   'John is fat'

A statement relating to past time would then have to be phrased something like 'some time ago John fat'.

There may be a copula which can be left out in certain conditions. For example, in Hungarian the copula is omitted in present tense when the CS is 3rd person and the CC relates to

Identity or Attribution (but is included when it relates to Possession or Location).

Some languages have several copulas as in English, *be* and also *become* 'getting into a relationship'. For example, *That man became a priest* and *John is becoming fat.* But note that *become* can only be used for Identity or Attribution, not for Possession, Benefactive, or Location. Spanish and Portuguese have two copulas: *ser* essentially refers to a permanent or semi-permanent state and *estar* to a temporary one.

If Paulo is a minister in the Brazilian government, one would normally describe this using *ser*:

Paulo é ministro   'Paul is a minister'

During a period of political upheaval in Brazil, when ministers seemed to succeed one another at a rapid rate, people would jokingly use *estar*:

Paulo está ministro 'Paul is a minister (here today, gone tomorrow)'

In summary, it is plainly useful to have a copula, rather than just relying on a verbless clause construction. And to have more than one copula adds a helpful nuance.

3.6 Succinctness

One could talk in short sentences, each consisting of a single clause. For example, in English:

(a)   John came in.
(b)   John saw this:

(c) The cat was eating the fish.

(d) Mary had left the fish lying on the table.

Every language has ways of integrating clauses into complex sentences, thus making an utterance more succinct. In the sample here, *John* recurs in (a) and (b), and *the fish* in (c) and (d), while (c) describes what John saw, in (b).

In view of this, (a–d) can be integrated into one complex sentence:

John came in and saw [that the cat was eating the fish [which Mary had left lying on the table]RELATIVE.CLAUSE]COMPLEMENT.CLAUSE

Clauses (a) and (b) are linked together, this being marked by coordinator *and*. Clause (a) has *John* in S (intransitive subject) function and (b) has *John* in A (transitive subject) function. The grammar of English allows *John* to be omitted from the second clause in these circumstances.

The O argument for verb *see*, as in (b), could be a noun phrase (*John saw the cat*) or, as here, it can be what is called a 'complement clause', describing an activity which John saw; the complement clause is introduced by *that—John saw [that the cat was eating the fish]*.

A noun such as *fish* can be modified by an adjective, which precedes it (*fresh fish*), or by a relative clause, which follows it. Both adjective and relative clause serve to narrow the reference of the head noun. Here the relative clause is introduced by *which— the fish [which Mary had left lying on the table]*.

Complement clause and relative clause constructions are said to involve 'subordination' since one clause is included within another. The subordinate clauses are 'dependent' on the main clause. Every language shows some techniques of subordination, although the details vary.

There can be a number of different types of complement clauses, each with its own meaning. There are three basic types in English:

- Describing a **fact**, marked by *that*, as in *I saw [that John had cooked the dinner]*.
- Describing an **activity**, marked by *-ing* on the verb of the complement clause, as in *I watched [John cooking the dinner]*.
- Describing some **potentiality** (purpose or intention), marked by *(for)...to*, as in *I had intended [(for) John to cook the dinner]* (but in fact Mary had done so before John arrived home).

Some languages have a single complement clause construction which covers all three meanings. Some have four or more with, say, different constructions for direct and indirect intention. Others have none at all and have to resort to relative clauses, something like 'I watched John who was cooking the dinner'.

The grammatical principles underlying subordinate clause constructions differ from language to language, and so do those for coordination. Some languages have an explicit marker for coordination, like *and* in English: *Mary came in and sat down*. Others—such as Dyirbal—simply juxtapose the two clauses: 'Mary came in, sat down'.

There is also an interesting difference between languages concerning the omission of arguments under coordination. In English, if two coordinated clauses share an argument and it is in S or A function in each clause, then it can be omitted from the second clause. Thus, confronted with

[The girl]$_A$ frightened [the woman]$_O$ and —$_S$ laughed

we understand that the S argument omitted from the second clause (at the position shown by '—') must have the same reference as the A argument in the first clause; that is, it was the girl who laughed.

We say that English has an 'S/A pivot' for coordination. This makes sense since in English S and A arguments are marked in the same way— both precede the verb and have the same form for pronouns (*I, he, she, we, they*). This can be compared with Dyirbal, where S and O are marked in the same way, by absolutive case which has zero realisation. We can repeat two of the Dyirbal sentences from section 3.4:

Yibi$_O$ nayi-nggu$_A$ marrba-ñu

woman   girl-ERGATIVE   frighten-PAST

'The girl frightened the woman'

Yibi$_S$ miyanda-ñu

woman   laugh-PAST

'The woman laughed'

In keeping with the fact that S and O arguments are marked in the same way, Dyirbal employs an 'S/O pivot'—if two coordinated clauses share an argument and it is in S or O function in each clause, then it can be omitted from the second clause. Thus, if one hears

Yibi$_O$ nayi-nggu$_A$ marrba-ñu —$_S$ miyanda-ñu

it is understood that the S argument omitted from the second clause (at '—') must have the same reference as the O argument in the first clause; that is, it was the woman who laughed. This sentence means 'The girl frightened the woman and the woman laughed'. The difference between English and Dyirbal is striking.

There can be several other kinds of clause linking. Many—but not all—languages have a marker of disjunction. In English, *or* may link words or phrases, or clauses, as in: *I heard a loud noise; it was a big truck on the highway or thunder rumbling in the distance.* Quite a few languages lack a disjunctive linker and instead add 'maybe' to each clause: 'Maybe it was a big truck on the highway, maybe it was thunder rumbling in the distance.'

Many languages spoken by small tribal groups lack a disjunctive linker. However, this is one of the first items they borrow, when brought into contact with a national language such as Spanish, Portuguese, or English. This surely shows that a marker of disjunction is a highly desirable feature for any language.

A variety of other types of linker are found in some—but again not in all—languages, including markers of consequence ('if'), cause ('because', 'therefore', 'and so'), and contrast ('but'). It is likely that every language has some means for indicating relative time ('after', 'before').

One ingenious technique for clause linking is 'switch reference'. This involves a pair of markers, one indicating that two clauses have the 'same subject' (argument in S or A function) and the other that they have 'different subjects'. This can be illustrated for Chickasaw, a Muskogean language from Oklahoma:

Baa'fa-cha   hõs-tok
stab-SAME.SUBJECT.LINKER   shoot-PAST
'He stabbed it and he (the same he) shot it'

Baa'fa-na   hõs-tok

stab-DIFFERENT.SUBJECT.LINKER   shoot-PAST

'He stabbed it and he (a different he) shot it'

Switch-reference markers may be added to the first of two clauses—which may be in a relation of coordination or subordination—or to the second, or sometimes to both. Interestingly, in all the languages for which switch reference has been reported, it relates to same/different S or A arguments, never S or O.

In summary, it is useful to employ an explicit marker of coordination ('and') rather than just juxtaposing clauses. A pivot condition for omitting repeated arguments is a handy device, S/A and S/O pivots being equally effective. Markers of disjunction, consequence, cause, contrast, and so on, are highly desirable.

There is considerable variation concerning types of subordination. One language may have several kinds of complement clause while another shows a rich variety of relative clauses. This makes it difficult to compare between languages.

Having surveyed features which recur in all languages, we can now go on to consider others, which are found in many languages.

Chapter 4

What is desirable

There are a number of grammatical systems which are found in many—but not in all—languages. They fulfil a useful function for languages in which they occur, and presumably could do so in every language. Just a selection is surveyed in this chapter: gender and classifiers (section 4.1), articles (4.2), tense, modality, and aspect (4.3), evidentiality (4.4), comparative constructions (4.5), passives, reflexives, and reciprocals (4.6), and causatives and applicatives (4.7).

4.1 Gender and classifiers

Language provides a tool for people to classify things in the world around them, and gender fulfils an important role in this practice.

Gender is a grammatical system, with a limited number of terms. Each noun in the language belongs to one gender (just a few nouns may relate to more than one). Gender may or may not be shown in the form of the noun itself. Irrespective of this, a criterion for grammatical gender is that it should be shown somewhere outside the noun itself. This may be through a

75

Are Some Languages Better than Others? First Edition. R. M. W. Dixon.
© R. M. W. Dixon 2016. Published 2016 by Oxford University Press.

modifier within the noun phrase, or through agreement on the verb.

In German, for instance, the gender of a noun (in singular number) is shown on an adjective or an article preceding it in the noun phrase:

der (masculine) Mann 'the man'
die (feminine) Frau   'the woman'
das (neuter) Buch   'the book'

In Jarawara, a verb takes suffixes some of which show the gender of the noun in subject function. For example declarative mood is -*ke* for feminine and -*ka* for masculine agreement. With verb *sona*- 'fall' we get:

Mati sona-ke   'Mother falls'
Bati sona-ka   'Father falls'

One discovers the gender of a noun in Jarawara by using it in a sentence. For example, *bahi* 'sun, thunder', *abariko* 'moon', and *amowa* 'star' all take declarative -*ka* and are thus masculine; they are regarded as legendary men. *Sami* 'pineapple' and *jifari* 'banana' take -*ke*, being classed under feminine. *Inamatewe* 'child' is one of the few nouns which take either of the two gender markers: *Inamatewe sona-ke* is 'A female child falls' while *Inamatewe sona-ka* is 'A male child falls'.

English does have sex-based 3rd person singular pronouns—*he*, *she*, and *it*—but does not satisfy the criterion for a grammatical category of gender. In this it differs from other familiar languages such as French, Spanish, and Welsh (which have two genders), and German, Russian, and Latin (which have three).

There is always some semantic basis for the grouping of nouns into genders. 'Masculine' and 'feminine' relate to male and female sex for humans, and for larger animals for which sex is significant. If there is a 'neuter' term, this will cover most inanimates, but there may be further semantic principles at work. In Latin, for example, the names of all winds and of most rivers and mountains are masculine, while the names of most islands, countries, cities, and trees are feminine.

The world hosts a multiplicity of objects, properties, states, actions, concepts, ideas. In contrast, every grammar has a compact format, with a limited number of categories, parameters, and construction types. As a consequence, one typically finds that several real-world distinctions are mapped onto a single grammatical contrast. This means that the set of words with a particular grammatical profile is likely to be heterogeneous.

Dyirbal has four genders; each noun may occur with an article, which shows its gender. The basic concepts associated with the genders are:

I   (article *bayi*)—male humans; non-human animates
II   (*balan*)—female humans; fire; drinkable liquids; fighting
III   (*balam*)—edible plant foods
IV   (*bala*) is then a residue gender, dealing with everything else
      (including body and other parts, place names, meat, and fish)

Some nouns are assigned a gender in terms of cultural association, rather than their inherent nature. As mentioned in section 1.5, 'sun' and 'moon' are believed to be wife and husband, hence 'sun' is in gender II, like human females, while 'moon' is in gender I, like males. Birds are believed to incorporate the spirits of dead human females and are thus in gender II.

If some subset of a general class of things has a special property, which sets it apart from the rest of the class, this may be highlighted by assigning it to another gender. Whereas most birds are in gender II, hawks are in gender I because 'they eat other birds'. Most snakes are—like other non-human animates—in gender I; but pythons constitute a special subset since they are the only snakes which are eaten; in recognition of this, they are placed in gender II.

Each of genders I and II includes several quite different things. Speakers emphasised to me that there is no connection between 'human females', 'fire', 'drinkable liquids', 'fighting', and 'edible snakes', for instance. This is why I do not employ labels such as 'feminine'. If such a label were adopted, there might be a temptation to make misleading statements such as: 'words relating to fire belong to feminine gender'. A more appropriate formulation is: 'words relating to fire and those describing human females belong to the same gender'.

The basic concepts and related semantic principles do explain the great majority of gender assignments in Dyirbal but—as in all such cases—not quite all of them. For example, I know of no reason why prawns and crabs, and also dogs, are in gender II.

Some gender systems can be larger, and do not always include a 'masculine/feminine' distinction. For instance, in Swahili (a Bantu language from East Africa), there are basically seven genders. There is a prefix on each noun, and on words modifying it within its noun phrase, and also on the verb, combining information on gender and also whether singular or plural reference. Quoting singular/plural prefix pairs, the rough meanings covered by four of the genders are:

m-/wa-   human beings (of both sexes)
m-/mi-   trees and plants and their useful products (except fruits)
ji-/ma-   things which occur in quantities (e.g. fruit, leaves, teeth)
ki-/vi-   many inanimate things; and diminutives

The following sentence shows how -*kombe* 'cup' takes *vi-*, the plural prefix for its *ki-/vi-* gender, and this is repeated on modifying adjective and number word, and on the verb:

Vi-kombe   vi-dogo   vi-wili   vi-mevunjika
vi-cup   vi-small vi-two   vi-broken
'Two small cups are broken'

When linguists began to investigate languages outside Europe, such as Swahili, the fact that there was no masculine/feminine distinction made them reluctant to employ the term 'gender', and 'noun classes' was used instead. In recent years, the term 'noun classes' has been dropped in favour of 'gender' (whether or not there are contrasting terms for male and female sexes).

Instead of a grammatical system of gender, some languages have a set of 'classifiers', nouns with a general meaning which occur in a noun phrase together with a noun which has more specific reference. For example, Yidiñ (Dyirbal's northerly neighbour) lacks genders but has around twenty classifiers. Their use can be seen in:

[Mayi   jimirr]$_O$ [bama-al   yaburu-nggu]$_A$ jula-al
vegetable   yam   person-ERGATIVE   girl-ERGATIVE   dig-PAST
'The person [CLASSIFIER] girl dug up the vegetable [CLASSIFIER] yam'

The specific noun *jimirr* 'yam' is accompanied by classifier *mayi* 'edible vegetable food' while *yaburu* 'girl' occurs with classifier

79

bama 'person'. It will be seen that classifier and specific noun make up one noun phrase and take the same case (see section 3.4). This is ergative for A (transitive subject) function, shown by suffix -*nggu* on *yaburu* 'girl' and irregular -*al* on *bama* 'person'; and absolutive case for O (transitive object) function, shown by a zero ending, as on *mayi* and *jimirr* here.

Whereas a gender system has a smallish number of terms (generally between two and ten), a classifier set may include scores of words. And whereas each noun must belong to a gender, classifiers only cover some specific nouns. In Yidiñ, for example, there are classifiers 'bird', 'frog', 'ant', 'tree', and 'vine', but nothing relating to kangaroos, snakes, or grasses.

In some languages, a number word must be accompanied by an appropriate classifier, determined by the nature of what is being counted. In Thai, for instance, classifier *mét* is used for counting small round objects such as grains, pills, or pimples; *kôon* for lumps, such as rocks and tofu; *múan* for rolled-up objects, such as tapes and toilet paper. Several other varieties of classifier are found across the languages of the world: some used in possessive constructions, some with verbs, indicating what type of object is in S (intransitive subject) or O (transitive object) function.

Some languages have a gender system, some have a set of classifiers, some have neither, and just a few have both. For instance, Malto (a Dravidian language from north-east India) has a masculine versus non-masculine gender system on demonstratives, and also a dozen or so classifiers, including *pula* for counting round light objects such as 'flower', 'mushroom', and 'cooked rice', *parta* for counting flat, broad objects such as 'cloud', 'cake', and 'tongue', and *panda* for counting long flexible objects such as 'rope', 'tail', and 'song'. For instance:

ti:ni ('three') panda (classifier) ca:me ('song'), 'three songs'

Genders and classifiers both serve to categorise the world within which a language is spoken, fulfilling similar semantic roles in rather different ways. It is definitely desirable that a language should include one or the other. Gender is the most useful since it is integrated into the grammar and can play a significant role in creating succinct discourse. This is illustrated in the next section.

4.2 Articles

In its widest sense, 'article' is used of several kinds of grammatical system whose members feature in a noun phrase. In Fijian (typical of Oceanic languages) each noun phrase must commence with one of two 'articles'. *Na* is used if the head of the phrase is a common noun, and *o* if it is a proper name (of a person or place) or a pronoun. Thus *na tamata* 'man', *na ika* 'fish', *o Jone* 'John', and *o iko* 'you'.

What I have been calling 'articles' in Dyirbal have three components. First there is *ba-* 'there', *ya-* 'here', or *nga-* 'not visible'. Then comes a case affix, similar to that on nouns: zero for absolutive, *-nggu* for ergative (ERG), etc. The final element shows the gender of the head noun: *-l* for gender I, *-n* for II, *-m* for the 'edible' gender III, and zero for IV. (There is one irregularity: gender I absolutive is *bayi* when *bal* would have been expected.) Unlike in Fijian an article is not obligatory in every noun phrase in Dyirbal, but it is included more often than not. An example sentence is

[Nga-n	yibi]$_O$	[ba-nggu-l	yara-nggu]$_A$	ngamba-n
NON.VISIBLE-II	woman	THERE-ERG-I	man-ERG	hear-PAST

'Man there heard woman who was not visible'

The narrow meaning of the label 'article' is for grammatical elements which mark a noun phrase as indefinite or definite (the 'articles' in Fijian and in Dyirbal do not do this). English has indefinite *a(n)*, used only with a singular countable noun, and definite *the*, used with all kinds of nouns, in both singular and plural number. Other languages may encode articles with information concerning gender and number, as in Portuguese:

	INDEFINITE	DEFINITE
masculine singular	um	o
feminine singular	uma	a
masculine plural	uns	os
feminine plural	umas	as

The singular indefinite article also functions as number 'one'.

Articles in the narrow sense are found in most of the languages of Europe and its immediate surrounds (although not, for instance, in Russian, Polish, or Finnish) but in few from elsewhere. Overall, less than one-tenth of world languages include an indefinite/ definite contrast coded through articles.

If so many languages get by without articles in the narrow sense, it behoves us to enquire what use they are. First, consider the English sentence:

We bought a dog and a cat but the dog died

The two occurrences of *a* in the first clause introduce the animals: we bought one from the set of all dogs and one from the set of all cats. In the second clause, *the* indicates a definite entity which the addressee is able to identify ('dog' from the first clause).

How could this be rendered in a language without articles? In effect, the article slots would simply be left empty, giving 'We bought dog and cat but dog died'. Unless something else were specified, one would assume that 'dog' in the second clause referred to the same animal as 'dog' in the first clause. In this instance, little would be lost for an article-less language.

Now consider the contrastive use of articles in:

(a)   Mary is the boss at the distillery
(b)   John is a boss at the factory

Definite article *the* before *boss* in sentence (a) indicates unique reference, stating that Mary is the top official. Indefinite article *a* before *boss* in sentence (b) simply says that John is one of a number of people in senior management positions at the factory.

This is where an article-less language runs into difficulties. Missing out articles from sentences (a) and (b) completely loses the meaning contrast, which must then be rendered by other means. One would have to say something like 'Mary is real top boss...' and 'John is one of bosses...'

An anecdote will illustrate the discourse potential of genders and articles. I entered a shop in the Brazilian city of Porto Velho to purchase a mirror (*um espelho*), which one of my Jarawara friends had asked me to bring him. The shopkeeper produced a box (*uma caixa*), extracted a mirror from it, and quoted the price:

Dez reais por uma   'Ten reais for one'

I protested that ten reais (about five dollars) was far too much for one small mirror. In true Brazilian fashion, the shopkeeper bargained himself down—nine reais, then eight. Still, I considered, far too much.

Then it hit me. My gender-starved brain has failed to pick up that he said *por uma*. The feminine form of the indefinite article (here functioning as the number 'one') must be referring to the box, *uma caixa*. The price being quoted was for a box of ten mirrors. If he had been giving the price for a mirror, *um espelho*, he would have said *por um*. I purchased one mirror, for one real, and left the shopkeeper shaking his head at foreigners who can't understand simple language.

If the transaction had been conducted in English, a price would have had to be quoted *for a box* or *for a mirror*. It can be seen that marking gender on articles in Portuguese makes for a more succinct discourse.

We can surely conclude that although only some languages have genders and only a few include articles marking indefinite/ definite, these are very useful features, and it is especially helpful when they are combined together.

4.3 Tense, modality, and aspect

Time is not symmetrical. The past is definite—generally, we know what has happened—the present is momentaneous, and the future is a mish-mash of possibilities and obligations. Note also that some statements are timeless, such as 'Pigs don't fly', 'Everyone loves Christmas', and 'The North Pole is cold'.

There are two ways of dealing with future time. Some languages have a straightforward system of three tenses—past, present, and future. These are 'shifters'; see section 2.5. Lithuanian is one language which has a basic three-tense system (plus a 'past habitual', for something which used often to happen). As in many other languages, 'present tense' is also employed for time-less statements.

If a 'future' term is included in a tense system, it basically indicates prediction ('I will drink milk'). But there are more possibilities relating to the future than this. The alternative to future tense is a set of 'modality' markers. English has a number of modal auxiliaries which precede the main verb. They include:

MODALITY	MODAL AUXILIARY	EXAMPLE
prediction	will	'It will rain tomorrow'
obligation	should	'I should attend the wedding (but may not be able to)'
necessity	must	'I must attend the wedding (come what may)'
possibility	may, might	'I may/might attend the wedding'
imminent activity	be about to	'I am about to vomit'
ability	can	'John can speak French'

Bini (from Nigeria) has particles coding some of the same modalities as English, and an additional one, 'desire':

MODALITY	MODAL PARTICLE	EXAMPLE
necessity	ghâ	'I must pay that debt'
imminent activity	khian	'We are about to sleep'
desire	gha	'I want to/will follow you'

In keeping with its use of modal particles to refer to the future, Bini has only two tenses—past and non-past.

English is often said to have two tenses. Suffix *-ed* (on regular verbs) does indeed refer to past time, as in *John painted a portrait.*

But suffix -*s* (for 3rd person singular subject) or zero (with other subjects) is not properly a present tense. Its uses include:

- For timeless and generic statements such as *John paints portraits* and *Dogs bark*.
- For use with a time word or phrase referring to the future, as in *We move to France next summer*, and *Father returns from his trip tomorrow*.

What about present time? English deals with it through the auxiliary *be* plus -*ing* on the following verb. This describes an activity that includes within its time span the present (which is just a moment); for example, *The dog is barking* and *John is painting a portrait*.

Grammarians have sometimes disputed over whether tense is a property of a clause or of a verb. It is best regarded as relating to both. Languages differ as to where in a sentence a tense marker is placed. Fijian has separate words—*na* for future and *aa* for past—which come between the subject pronoun and the verb. With 1st person singular pronoun *au* and verb *lako* 'go', we get:

Au na lako   'I will go'
Au aa lako   'I went'
Au lako   'I am going'

Note that present activity is here shown by leaving the tense slot blank.

Tense markers in Fijian are optional and used only as needed. Typically, a future or past marker is included just in the first clause of a narrative. This establishes the time frame, which is assumed to hold for all that follows (or until a new tense marker is stated).

However most languages do code tense on the verb, and a tense choice must then be indicated for each clause. There is sometimes a portmanteau affix which combines information on tense with other grammatical categories. Latin provides an extreme example of this; for example, the ending -*at* on verb *amat* 'he/she loves/is loving' combines present tense with 3rd person singular subject, active voice, and declarative mood.

The number of terms in a tense system varies. There may be the standard three, but more common is a two-term system; this is most often past/non-past but there are some instances of future/non-future. Some languages have several past tenses, referring to different lengths of time before the present moment. The three past tenses in Jarawara were mentioned in section 2.1—immediate past for anything which happened from a moment ago to a few months in the past, recent past for from a few months to a few years ago, and far past for a more distant event.

There may also be several future tenses. For example, Washo (spoken in Nevada) has four pasts and three futures, shown by the following suffixes:

-leg	earlier today or last night
-ay?	yesterday or a little earlier
-gul	within the speaker's lifetime
-lul	before the speaker was born
-ásha?	in the immediate future, for up to a few hours from now
-ti?	more than a few hours distant, but still within today
-gab	tomorrow or any time later

I know of no languages with tense distinctions in the future but none in the past, nor of any with more distinctions in future than in past.

Note that, if there is a tense system, this applies in declarative clauses and generally in all kinds of interrogatives but not in imperatives. As mentioned in section 3.1, there may be a rather different contrast in commands, between 'Do it now!' and 'Do it in some other place or time!' Quite a number of languages lack a grammatical system of tense. There will always be lexical time words such as 'yesterday' and 'later on'. And there may be other kinds of grammatical specification. For example, in Tagalog (a major Austronesian language, spoken in the Philippines), each verb must make a choice from a three-term system, whose members indicate:

- activity completed
- activity begun but not completed
- activity contemplated

Slavic languages employ a grammatical system relating to extent in time. This has two members:

- 'perfective'—an event is regarded as a whole without regard for its temporal composition (even though it may be extended in time)
- 'imperfective'—this focuses on the temporal make-up of an event

Russian has a system of three tenses—past, present, and future—interrelating with specification for perfective/imperfective. An illustration of how this works is:

Poka	Ivan	spal,		Masha	vymyla		pol
while	Ivan	slept:IMPERFECTIVE		Masha	washed:PERFECTIVE		floor

'While Ivan was sleeping, Masha washed the floor'

Ivan's sleeping is here described as an activity extended in time, and Masha's washing the floor as a unit event which took place during Ivan's sleeping.

The term 'aspect' was first used to describe the perfective/imperfective contrast in Slavic languages but is now often employed for various systems—other than tense—associated with the verb. For example, that just described for Tagalog. Or for 'telicity', where 'telic' describes an activity with a definite endpoint (such as 'Mary sang Waltzing Matilda') and 'atelic' is used of an activity which does not have any definite conclusion ('John is singing bawdy songs in the bar').

In summary, communication is assisted by the grammar including a tense system. Reference to what has not yet happened may be through a future tense or, alternatively, by means of a set of modality markers; the latter is more informative and thus to be preferred. Other specifications—such as several past and perhaps also future tenses, and various kinds of aspect systems—can be regarded as luxuries which may be indulged in to the extent that they can be accommodated within the language's limits of overall complexity; see chapter 8.

Linguistic terminology can be confusing. 'Mood', referring to types of speech act (declarative, imperative, interrogative), is a totally different thing from 'modality', describing aspects of the future (obligation, possibility, prediction, etc.). Care must also be taken to distinguish between 'perfective'/'imperfective' and the quite different 'perfect/imperfect'. The term 'perfect' refers to an event which is completed but still has present relevance, and 'imperfect' to something which began in the past and is still continuing.

4.4 Evidentiality

In a responsible society, it is important to be careful about what is said. How do you know it? By direct evidence? Because you were told? Or is it just a hunch?

A grammatical system of 'evidentiality' (found in about a quarter of the world's languages) specifies the source of information on which a statement is based. The size of the system varies from just two terms in some languages to half-a-dozen (or maybe more) in others.

As described in section 2.1, each of the three past tenses in Jarawara has two evidentiality values. There is an obligatory choice between them. One morning I came out of my hut in the Jarawara village and noticed that a tree, *awa* (feminine gender), had fallen (verb *sona-*) in the night. I said, using feminine forms of the immediate past suffix (*-hare*) and declarative suffix (*-ke*):

Awa sona-hara-ke   'The tree has fallen over'

This was at once corrected. Although I saw that the tree had fallen. I did not actually witness it toppling over, which is what was implied by what I had said, using *-hara*, the eyewitness form of immediate past feminine. I should have employed the non-eyewitness form *-hani*:

Awa sona-hani-ke
'The tree has fallen over (I didn't see it happen)'

Estonian has a two-term evidentiality system of a different nature. There is an obligatory choice between 'reported', when you were told about something, and 'non-reported', for something known directly, as in:

| Elsa | on | ilus | 'Elsa is beautiful (I know it)' |
| Elsa | is:NON.REPORTED | beautiful | |

| Elsa | olevat | ilus | 'Elsa is beautiful (they say)' |
| Elsa | is:REPORTED | beautiful | |

Both the Jarawara and Estonian contrasts are included within larger evidentiality systems, such as that for Tariana, which has five terms. Their meanings, and forms in recent past tense are:

	EVIDENTIALITY VALUES (with central meanings)	RECENT PAST
1	VISUAL: speaker has seen it, or speaker takes full responsibility for statement	-ka
2	NON-VISUAL: speaker has heard, smelt, tasted, or felt (but not seen) it; for example, a phone ringing	-mahka
3	INFERRED: not seen but inferred from specific evidence	-nihka
4	ASSUMED: not seen, but inferred on the basis of general knowledge	-sika
5	REPORTED: when someone else informed the speaker of it	-pidaka

Example sentences are (with verb -pita- 'wash', 3rd singular masculine bound pronoun prefix di-, and recent past suffixes in the five evidentiality values):

1 Jose di-pita-ka   'Jose has washed (I saw him doing it)'
2 Jose di-pita-mahka 'Jose has washed (I heard him splashing about)'

3 Jose di-pita-nihka   'Jose has washed (I see wet footprints and a sodden towel)'

4 Jose di-pita-sika   'Jose has washed (it is dinner time and I know that he always washes just before dinner)'

5 Jose di-pita-pidaka   'Jose has washed (someone told me)'

The maximum number of evidentiality choices is likely to be in past tense for declarative mood. There tend to be fewer in present tense and fewer still (if any) in future. The five-term system in Tariana applies only for remote past and recent past tenses; present tense has just three choices (omitting inferred and assumed), and there is no evidentiality specification in future.

Interrogative mood generally allows a smaller selection of choices. For Tariana there are three for past tense interrogatives—visual, non-visual, and inferred—and just two in present tense—visual and non-visual. The only contrast in imperatives is direct ('Come and eat!') versus reported ('Come and eat as you were told to do!').

Languages without an evidentiality system in the grammar can of course employ lexical means to obtain a similar effect, albeit awkwardly—*It is reported that the alleged murderer was seen in Central Park*. But things lexical are always optional. Evidentiality as a grammatical system is an obligatory specification. One cannot, in Tariana, just say 'John washed'; the evidence on which this statement is based must be provided. If we had such obligatory specification in English, wouldn't this be a boon for the police? And an embarrassment for evasive politicians?

Evidentials allow double possibilities for fibbing. One can either lie about what happened, or lie about the evidence used.

For example, saying *Jose di-pita-ka*, 'Jose has washed (I saw him doing it)', either when you know he hasn't washed or when you were only told about it and didn't witness it yourself.

In summary, an evidentiality system is a most useful inclusion in any grammar, with as many values as the overall complexity of the grammar can accommodate.

4.5 Comparative constructions

The book you are reading is an attempt at a comparative study. Surely nothing could be more natural? In the western world, where I was reared, people vie to see who is fastest, cleverest, strongest, most beautiful. We award prizes for being best at this and at that, applaud it, bet on it.

However, not every society is like this. In the traditional culture of Dyirbal speakers, from North Queensland, and of the Jarawara, from southern Amazonia (two groups with whom I have had a close acquaintance), there was no factor of competitiveness. The vocabularies include no words which could render 'compete', 'win', 'lose', 'victory', or 'victor'.

By the time I first visited the Jarawara (in the early 1990s), they had adopted the Brazilian national game of soccer, played on a makeshift pitch at the end of the missionary airstrip. When, in my competitive-culture way, I enquired about the score, the answer always was 'It's equal'. They played for the fun of scoring goals and didn't count them. Ten years later, acculturation had crept up and the score was being kept, but using words taken from Portuguese.

Such peoples did not indulge in comparison for its own sake. There were, of course, utilitarian judgements such as 'This container is better than that one since it has a handle' or, when explaining the locations of villages: 'A is not far, B is quite far, and C is further'. But I never encountered comparative evaluations concerning people. Jarawara and Dyirbal did not include fully-fledged comparative constructions in their grammars simply because their cultural make-up did not require them.

For larger societies, in which competitiveness provides a major motivation ('I want to be top of the class', 'Mary is the highest-grossing salesperson in the business'), the grammar should make suitable provision. The prototypical comparative scheme can be illustrated from English, with its elements labelled:

Tom	is	more	generous	than	Harry
COMPAREE	INDEX	PARAMETER		MARK	STANDARD

There are two participants in this evaluation—*Tom* is being compared with *Harry*, who is here the 'standard of comparison'. They are being compared in terms of a property (*generous*) which is the 'parameter of comparison'. The parameter is in most languages (though not in all) accompanied by an 'index', here *more* (an alternative would be *less*). And there may be a grammatical item marking the standard, as *than* does here.

There are different techniques of comparison in other languages. For example 'Tom's strength exceeds Harry's strength', and 'Tom exceeds Harry, Tom is tall' (meaning 'Tom is taller than Harry'). However, there are quite a few languages—in competitive societies—lacking a full-fledged comparative construction. One simply has to extrapose two clauses, saying something like: 'Tom is tall; Harry is not tall' or 'Harry is tall; Tom is very tall'.

Comparison can involve gradation—'more than' and 'less than'—or identity—'the same as'. It is perhaps unsurprising that languages such as Dyirbal and Jarawara, which have no need of comparative constructions, do express identity. One can say 'My house is the same (design) as your house'. A Jarawara man who was soon to depart remarked: 'My sleepings are the same as two of our hands', meaning 'I have ten more nights'.

The standard comparative construction can be extended in various ways. For example, two properties can be compared in relation to one participant, as in *This box is longer than it is wide*. Or both 'comparee' and 'standard' may be clauses, as in:

[John speaks French] better than [Mary speaks German]

And we can create somewhat extravagant comparisons such as:

[Tom likes Ibsen] more than [Mary hates Kafka]

In summary, it is certainly a good thing, in the language of a society which values competition, to have an explicit comparative construction, although it is not necessary for it to stretch as far as the English sentence just quoted.

4.6 Passives, reflexives, and reciprocals

As described in section 3.4, a transitive clause has two core arguments and an intransitive clause has one. Many languages include techniques for converting a transitive clause into an intransitive construction—passive, and one variety of reflexive and of reciprocal. There may also be techniques for converting an intransitive clause into a transitive one—causative and applicative; these are discussed in section 4.7.

A transitive clause has core arguments in A (transitive subject) and O (transitive object) functions, as in *John$_A$ ate [the cake]$_O$.*

For some transitive verbs in English the noun phrase in O function may be omitted in suitable circumstances; for example, one can say *John is eating* or *John ate an hour ago*.

However, a noun phrase in A function can never be omitted; it is not permissible to say *Ate the cake* or *Is eating the cake*. There is a crafty way of dealing with this—employ a passive derivation. Passive applies to a transitive clause, is marked by *-en* or *-ed* on the verb and *be* (which carries tense), before it, and puts the original O argument into S (intransitive subject) function within a derived intransitive construction: *[The cake]$_S$ was eaten yesterday*. The original A argument can be included, now marked with *by*—*[The cake]$_S$ was eaten (by John) yesterday*—but is omitted in the great majority of instances.

Passive has many uses, including:

(a) When the identity of the underlying A argument is not known—as in *John was attacked last night*—or is not important—*The cake was eaten yesterday*.

(b) To focus on the result of an activity, as in *John was wounded*.

(c) To allow a topic to run through a series of clauses. For example, *The assassin threw down his gun, ran off, and hid in a barn for two days before being apprehended* (to substitute for the last clause *before the police apprehended him* would make the narrative disjointed).

(d) To allow a repeated noun phrase to be omitted, creating a tighter discourse.

As explained in section 3.6, English operates in terms of an S/A pivot: if two coordinated clauses share an argument and it is in S or A function in each clause, then it can be omitted from the second clause. One can thus link together *John$_S$ came in* and *John$_A$ saw Mary$_O$* as:

John$_S$ came in and—$_S$ saw Mary$_O$

However, given John$_S$ came in and Mary$_A$ saw John$_O$, we cannot omit John from the second clause since it is in O (not in A or S) function. That is, we cannot say John$_S$ came in and Mary$_A$ saw —$_O$. Passive comes to the rescue here. The transitive clause Mary$_A$ saw John$_O$ is made into passive (and intransitive) John$_S$ was seen by Mary. We now have John in pivot (S or A) function in each clause, so that it can be omitted from the second:

John$_S$ came in and —$_S$ was seen by Mary

Many—but far from all—languages have one or more passive constructions, typically marked by a derivational affix to the verb. Some have what is called an 'agentless passive' in which the A argument of the underlying transitive—rendered with a by-phrase in English—cannot be included.

Alongside languages, like English, with an S/A pivot for clause combining, section 3.6 mentioned languages, like Dyirbal, which work in terms of an S/O pivot. Such languages may have an 'antipassive' construction which places the underlying A argument into derived S function, and dispatches the original O into a peripheral function, from which it can be omitted. This assists clause linking on an S/O basis.

For some transitive verbs it is highly unlikely that the A and O arguments would be identical; these include 'precede', 'contain', 'learn', 'resemble'. For others, A and O sometimes do coincide—'cut', 'burn', 'see' (in a mirror or river), 'hear' (in a recording or an echo). To deal with this, many languages have reflexive constructions, which are of two main types.

(1) Maintain a transitive clause and place a reflexive pronoun in the O slot. In English this reflects the person and number of the A argument, as in *You*$_A$ *have burnt yourself*$_O$, and *[Members of the dance troop]*$_A$ *saw themselves*$_O$ *on TV*. Some languages have an invariant reflexive pronoun—literally, 'You have burnt self'.

(2) Create an intransitive clause by adding a reflexive affix to the verb. The original A = O argument now becomes S argument of the intransitive reflexive construction. This can be illustrated for the Girramay dialect of Dyirbal, where singular pronouns have different forms for the three core functions: 1st singular is *ngaja* for A, *ngayba* for S, and *ngaña* for O function. A straightforward transitive sentence (with verb *bura-* 'see' and past tense -*n*) is:

Ngaja$_A$ Jani$_O$ bura-n   'I saw John'

For reflexive, derivational suffix -*rri*- is added to the verb and past tense is now -*ñu*:

Ngayba$_S$ bura-rri-ñu (bana-ngga)   'I saw myself (in the water)'

Some languages do not have a reflexive construction; one just has to say 'You burnt you', and so on. This is alright for 1st and 2nd persons but can lead to difficulties in the case of 3rd person. On hearing 'Tom and Bill were cooking and Tom burnt him', one could not tell whether 'him' referred to 'Tom' or to 'Bill'. There can be a variant on this pattern, where the relevant body part is generally included in the O argument. In Jarawara, for instance, one would say 'You burnt your hand' and 'He saw his face (in the mirror)'.

If we have two clauses which are identical except that A and O are interchanged, this indicates reciprocal activity; for example, 'Tom$_A$ punched Bill$_O$' and 'Bill$_A$ punched Tom$_O$'. Many languages describe this through a reciprocal construction. There are two main varieties, similar to reflexives.

(1) A reciprocal pronoun in the O slot of transitive clause. This is generally invariable, as in English: *[John and Tom]$_A$ punched [each other]$_O$*.

(2) A derived intransitive construction, with reciprocal marking on the verb, and the S argument being the sum of A and O arguments in the underlying transitive clauses. That can also be illustrated from Dyirbal, with verb *bijil-* 'punch' and 1st person dual pronoun *ngali*. Reciprocal is shown by repetition of the first two syllables of the verb (known as 'reduplication') and derivational suffix *-nbarri-*.

Ngali$_S$ bijil-bijil-nbarri-ñu   'We two punched each other'

The meaning of 'reciprocal' is somewhat fluid. If someone says *The boys are punching each other*, this does not imply that every boy is both puncher and punchee with respect to every other boy. It just means that there is a good deal of punching going on, with some boys inflicting blows, some receiving them, with these two sets probably overlapping.

In many languages, reflexive and reciprocal are both rendered by technique (1)—as in English—or both by technique (2)—as in Dyirbal. Some have the pronoun construction for reflexive and the verbal derivation for reciprocal, never (to my knowledge) the reverse.

We sometimes find the same marking for reflexive and reciprocal. They may then only be distinguished in terms of the
number reference of the subject argument—singular must
mean reflexive, while plural generally indicates reciprocal. For
instance, in the Australian language Guugu Yimidhirr, with verb
gunda- 'hit', reflexive/reciprocal verbal suffix *-adhi*, and S arguments 1st person singular *ngayu* and 3rd person dual *bula*:

Ngayu$_S$ gunda-adhi   'I hit myself'
Bula$_S$ gunda-adhi   'The two of them hit each other'

In fact, the second sentence is likely to have a reciprocal meaning,
but it could be plural reflexive: 'Each of the two of them hit
himself or herself'.

In summary, it is extremely useful to have a passive derivation
(or an antipassive in the case of a language with an S/O pivot for
clause linking). It is also beneficial to include in the grammar
reflexive and reciprocal constructions—of either pronominal or
derived intransitive type—preferably with different markings.

4.7 Causatives and applicatives

An intransitive clause has one core argument and a transitive
clause two. There are thus two ways in which an intransitive
clause can be converted into a transitive one:

- S becomes O; new argument in A function—this is a 'causative'.
- S becomes A; new argument in O function—this is an 'applicative'.

In a causative, an original S argument goes into O function and a
new argument is introduced in A function, the 'causer'. The

causative construction is often marked by an affix to the intransitive verb, such as *as-* in Amharic (a Semitic language from Ethiopia). A basic intransitive clause is, with verb *č'əffərə-* 'dance', and bound pronoun suffix *-čč* indicating 3rd person feminine singular S:

Aster$_S$ č'əffərə-čč   'Aster danced'

Adding causative prefix *as-* to the verb, and 'causer' argument *Lemma*, in A function, we get:

Ləmma$_A$ Aster$_O$ as-č'əffərə-ø-at   ' Lemma made Aster dance'

In this transitive clause there is a zero suffix (shown as *-ø-*) for 3rd singular masculine A, and suffix *-at* for 3rd singular feminine O.

An alternative to having a special affix is to show causation through a periphrastic conduction, as English does with verb *make* (and also *force, cause, tempt*)—*Lemma made Aster dance*.

There may be a pair of verbs, one effectively the causative of the other. This can be illustrated by *go in* and *put in* for English; corresponding to *The dog went into the kennel* we have causative *John put the dog into the kennel*.

In some languages a causative construction may only involve intransitive verbs. In others it also applies to transitives—sometimes all, other times just a few, the most common being 'eat' and 'drink'.

There may be contrasting causative constructions, always with a meaning difference. In Hindi, suffix *-a* indicates that the causer acts directly and *-va* that they act indirectly. The intransitive clause (a) is the basis for the direct causative in (b), where the labourers did the job themselves, and for the indirect causative in (c), where the contractor achieved the task indirectly (through 'the labourers', who can be included in the clause, marked by instrumental case).

(a) Məkan_S   bəna
    house   was.made
    The house got built

(b) [Məzduuro ne]_A   makan_O bənay-a
    labourers ERGATIVE house   was.made-DIRECT.CAUSATIVE
    The labourers built the house

(c) [Thekedar ne]_A   (məzduuro se)   makan_O
    contractor ERGATIVE labourers INSTRUMENTAL house
    bənva-ya
    was.made-INDIRECT.CAUSATIVE
    The contractor got the house built (by the labourers)

A quite different semantic contrast is found in Kammu, an Austroasiatic language from Laos. If the causer achieves the result intentionally causative prefix *p-* is used, and if they achieve the result accidentally causative particle *tòk* is placed before the verb. Compare:

Kəə_A   p-háan   tráak_O
3sg:MASCULINE INTENTIONAL.CAUSATIVE-die buffalo
He slaughtered the buffalo (deliberately)

Kəə_A   tòk   háan múuc_O
3sg:MASCULINE UNINTENTIONAL.CAUSATIVE die   ant
He happened to kill an ant (e.g. by accidentally treading on it)

Other varieties of contrasting causative constructions can relate to whether or not the causee acted willingly ('He got her to dance and she was happy to do so' versus 'He forced her to dance when she didn't really want to'), or to whether or nor the causer also joined in the activity ('He made his son cross the river, and stayed on the bank watching' versus 'He made his son cross the river, and went across as well, helping him along'). And there are more besides.

Not every language has causatives. In Dyirbal, for instance, there is nothing corresponding to *Mary made John cry* in English. One has to be more specific and state what Mary did to bring on the tears. Perhaps 'Mary hit John so that he cried' or 'Mary told John that his father had died, and he cried' or, in directing a dramatic performance, 'Mary told John to cry'.

Applicatives have a quite different profile from causatives. Basically, an applicative takes a peripheral argument and places it in core function O. If the underlying clause was intransitive, its S argument takes on A function within the transitive applicative construction.

This can be illustrated from Dyirbal. *Mañja-* is an intransitive verb meaning 'eat to satisfy an aching hunger'. A peripheral noun phrase referring to what is eaten may optionally be added—here *wuray* 'Davidson plum' with instrumental suffix *-ju*:

Jani$_S$ mañja-ñu (wuray-ju)   'John ate (of Davidson plum)'

When applicative suffix *-ma-* is added to the verb, it creates a transitive construction in which the erstwhile optional peripheral argument *wuray* 'Davidson plum' is now in O function (and obligatory). *Jani*, 'John', goes into A function, marked by ergative suffix *-nggu*:

Jani-nggu$_A$ wuray$_O$ mañjay-ma-n   'John ate Davidson plum'

(Past tense is *-ñu* on verb root *mañja(y)-* and *-n* after applicative suffix *-ma-*.)

Placing a peripheral argument into a core function enables it to take part in clause linking. Suppose that there was a coordination: 'Tom$_A$ gathered Davidson plum$_O$ and John$_A$ ate (to assuage his hunger) the Davidson plum$_O$'. As explained in section 3.6, Dyirbal works in terms of an S/O pivot—if two coordinated clauses share an argument and it is in S or O function in each clause, then it can be omitted from the second clause. Putting *wuray* 'Davidson plum' into O function, within an applicative construction, makes it available for ellipsis.

An applicative derivation may also apply to a transitive clause. Once again, a peripheral argument is placed in O function. The A argument stays as is, and the original O argument is now outlawed into the periphery. This can be illustrated from Javanese (an Austronesian language). We commence with a transitive clause which has an optional instrumental noun phrase:

Sri$_A$ nuthuk   Bambang$_O$ (nganggo   garisan   iku)
Sri   hit   Bambang   WITH   ruler   THAT
'Sri hit Bambang (with that ruler)'

Applying the instrumental applicative suffix *-ake* to the verb strips 'that ruler' of its preposition and places it in O function. The original O argument, Bambang, is now marked by preposition *marang* 'to':

Sri$_A$ nuthuk-ake [garisan iku]$_O$ [marang Bambang]

Sri hit-APPLICATIVE ruler THAT TO Bambang

'Sri hit that ruler on (literally 'to') Bambang'

Whereas the great majority of languages include some sort of causative, only around one quarter have an applicative construction. A number do have several varieties of applicative, according to the original function of the peripheral argument which is to become O. Javanese, for instance, has four. Besides the instrumental applicative (just illustrated), there is locative ('He wrote Javanese script on the gate'), benefactive ('She cooked a cake for father'), and recipient ('He taught English to Bambang'). In each instance, the underlined argument is divested of its preposition and taken into O slot.

In summary, a causative construction is a most valuable asset, and it can be handy to have several of them, with contrasting meanings. Applicative constructions have a more limited role, basically moving what was originally a non-central component into focus.

Chapter 5
What is not (really) needed

The last two chapters have examined grammatical features which recur in all languages—and can thus be considered necessary—plus several which are found each in a fair number of languages—and appear, on the whole, to be desirable.

Not every aspect of human languages is ideal, or conducive to easy communication. This chapter examines complexities which appear at first sight to fulfil no useful role, and indeed to impede the efficient learning and use of languages. We look at irregularities in general (section 5.1), suppletion (5.2). grammatical and semantic redundancies (5.3–4), and a disallowance of repetition (5.5). They are all, in one sense, unnecessary. But is each of them really useless? This is a question which will be considered.

5.1 Irregularities

In a language which is truly streamlined, all nouns take the same set of affixes, similarly for all adjectives, and for all verbs. In English, regular plural marker is suffix -s. The few exceptions are gradually reducing: *kine* has been replaced by *cow-s* and *brethren* by *brother-s* (except in a religious context). Just a handful of

Are Some Languages Better than Others? First Edition. R. M. W. Dixon.
© R. M. W. Dixon 2016. Published 2016 by Oxford University Press.

irregularities remain, including *children, men,* and *mice* (although *mouse-s* is sometimes used for the computer artefact).

There are thousands of regular verbs in English, each of which has four forms:

1   Basic form, e.g. *join*
2   Add *-s* (3rd person singular subject 'present' tense): *join-s*
3   Add *-ing* (after 'progressive' *be*, and in participles): *join-ing*
4   Add *-ed* (past tense, after passive *be*, and after *have*): *join-ed*

English also has more than a hundred verbs which are irregular with respect to form 4. Indeed, some divide this up; for example:

1   Basic forms: *sew, speak, begin*
4a Past tense: *sewed, spoke, began*
4b Form used after passive *be* and after *have*: *sewn, spoken, begun*

Each irregular verb is more-or-less a law unto itself. We can compare:

	1 basic	4a	4b
REGULAR	greet	greet-ed	
IRREGULAR	eat	ate	eaten
	beat		beaten
	meet	met	

	1 basic	4a	4b
	wing	wing-ed	
	sing	sang	sung
	sting	stung	
	bring	brought	

In the left-hand table, basic forms all end with /iːt/ (spelled as *eet* or as *eat*) and in the right-hand table all end in *-ing*, yet the forms

108

in columns 4a and 4b are quite different and could not have been predicted from the basic form. Note that 4a = 4b for *meet, sting,* and *bring*, and 1= 4a for *beat*. Other irregular verbs show further possibilities, including 1 = 4b for *come*, and 1 = 4a = 4b for *hit* and *cut*.

These irregularities fulfil no communicative role. Past tense is past tense whether it is shown by *-ed/-d*, or by vowel change (as in *eat/ate* and *sing/sang*), or by a combination of these (*sell/sold*). Native and foreign language learners have to memorise all the irregularities when their minds would be better occupied in assimilating those parts of the grammar which carry contrasts of meaning. In a nutshell, irregularities constitute useless complications which are most definitely not needed.

It could be argued that irregularities assist in identifying people who are not native speakers. A foreign learner may perfectly master the pronunciation of, say, English but not be in total command of every grammatical nuance. The more complicated the grammar—and the more irregularities there are—the more chance there is of a native speaker catching out a foreigner: maybe they'll say *I have bended the wire*, rather than using *bent*. This may provide a social usefulness for irregularities, but it does not alter the fact that they are a communicative impedance.

Irregularities typically arise from sound changes, often at different times in the past. The language is, in a sense, encapsulating its history. This is interesting but unhelpful with respect to the functions a language has in the here-and-now. If English made every verb regular (saying *speak-ed* in place of *spoke* and *spoken*, and so on) it would certainly be less quaint, but a good deal more efficient.

When, in the early 1990s, I resolved to undertake fieldwork in Brazil—to investigate the grammar of Jarawara—a first step was to acquire at least a rudimentary competence in Portuguese. My teacher, from Brasilia, was concerned to instruct me in the correct grammar. Weekly lessons seemed mostly to be concerned with intricacies of verb structure. There are seven tense-aspect paradigms in declarative mood and three more in the subjunctive, each with a distinct form for three persons and two numbers of the subject. That's sixty forms to master. Besides the many regular verbs, there are several score irregular ones; since these are amongst the most common verbs, they must be mastered. A sample (from my textbook) of infinitive and present tense forms for one regular and three important irregular verbs is:

| | REGULAR VERB | | IRREGULAR VERBS | |
	'watch'	'see'	'hear'	'know'
infinitive	espi-ar	ver	ouvir	saber
1sg present	espi-o	vejo	ouço	sei
2sg present	espi-as	vês	ouves	sabes
3sg present	espi-a	vê	ouve	sabe
1pl present	espi-amos	vemos	ouvimos	sabemos
2pl present	espi-ais	vêdes	ouvis	sabeis
3pl present	espi-am	vêem	ouvem	sabem

Multiply this by many. I'd spent umpteen hours attempting to learn irregularities (rather than more useful, meaning-bearing, aspects of the grammar). And all to no avail, as it turned out.

The Jarawara had learnt something of the local variety of rural Portuguese, which is radically different from what I had been taught. The complexities of irregular verbs had been dealt with by simply eliminating many of them. Instead of irregular *ver* 'see', the regular verb *espiar* was employed (its original meaning was 'watch, observe, spy on'). In place of irregular *ouvir* 'hear' they used regular *escutar* (originally 'listen to').

The Jarawara had gone one step further by doing away with suffixes indicating person and number of subject. They adopted what had been the 3rd person singular form for use with every type of subject, this being indicated by a free pronoun—thus *Eu espia* 'I see' in place of *espio* (which was in turn in place of *vejo*). There was, as far as I could see, a single exception: my *Eu sabe* 'I know' was firmly corrected to *Sei*. Just for this verb, the 1st singular form had been retained.

Away from the confines of traditional literacy-bound ortho-doxy, a more rational framework had evolved for the local dialect of Portuguese. But this was soon forgotten as I became immersed in Jarawara and explored its own deep trove of irregularities.

In Jarawara an 'inalienably possessed' noun simply follows its possessor. Each non-possessed noun belongs to one of the two genders, feminine and masculine. About half of the possessed nouns have separate feminine and masculine forms, reflecting the gender of the possessor noun. For example, 'face' has femin-ine form *noki* and masculine *noko*. With possessors *mati* 'mother' and *bati* 'father' we get:

mati noki 'mother's face'   bati noko 'father's face'

Possessed nouns refer to parts of people, animals, and plants. and also to 'smell', 'dream', 'path (associated with a particular person)', and much more. About sixty-five of them have distinct feminine and masculine forms, but there is considerable vari-ation as to how the gender contrast is marked. Consider the following selection (there are several more possessed nouns relating to each row):

		FEMININE	MASCULINE
(a)	'face'	noki	noko
(b)	'cord'	mati	mato-ne
(c)	'voice'	ati	ati
(d)	'path'	hawi	hawi-ne
(e)	'stalk'	ate	ete
(f)	'foot'	tame	teme
(g)	'blood'	ame	eme-ne

In rows (a–b), feminine/masculine are distinguished by the second vowel, *i/o*. But in (e–g) the second vowel is always *e*, with gender being shown by the first vowel, *a/e*. For (c) there is no gender contrast. Just in rows (b), (d), and (g), masculine form bears suffix *-ne* (this being the only gender distinction in (d)).

There is no regular process for creating gender forms of possessed nouns in present-day Jarawara. The whole thing is wildly irregular. There is a sort of aesthetic charm to it. However, from the point of view of communicative efficiency, it is completely useless.

Irregular systems evolve from regular ones. By comparing forms in Jarawara with corresponding ones in sibling languages from the small Arawá family, gender marking on possessed nouns can be reconstructed for proto-Arawá, the ancestor language (these being marked by *). At that stage, everything was completely regular—gender suffixes *-ni* for feminine and *-ne* for masculine were added to invariable roots *noko*, *mato*, *ati*, *hawi*, *ate*, *tama*, and *ama*. Then the following changes took place:

		FEMININE			MASCULINE		
(a)	'face'	*noko-ni	>	noki	*noko-ne	>	noko
(b)	'cord'	*mato-ni	>	mati	*mato-ne	>	mato-ne

112

(c)	'voice'	*ati-ni	>	ati	*ati-ne	>	ati
(d)	'path'	*hawi-ni	>	hawi	*hawi-ne	>	hawi-ne
(e)	'stalk'	*ate-ni	>	ate	*ate-ne	>	ete
(f)	'foot'	*tama-ni	>	tame	*tama-ne	>	teme
(g)	'blood'	*ama-ni	>	ame	*ama-ne	>	eme-ne

Suffix -*ni* has been completely lost from feminine forms, but some traces remain. In rows (a–b), *-oni* is relaced by -*i*, and in rows (f–g), *-ani* becomes -*e*. Following -*i* and -*e*, in rows (c–e), -*ni* is simply dropped.

Masculine suffix -*ne* has been dropped from some possessed nouns but is retained with others (I have not been able to detect any principle underlying this). When -*ne* followed *a*, it caused this *a*, and any preceding *a*'s, to become *e*, in (f–g). For row (e), the two following *e*'s made the *a* in the first syllable assimilate to *e*.

Everything can be explained, but this doesn't make it easier to master the intricacies of the modern language. Why did these changes take place? To produce shorter words (*noki* rather than *nokoni*), or words with the same vowel all through, making for easier pronunciation (*emene* instead of *amane*). But phonological simplification came at the cost of obscuring the original rational principles for gender assignment. The language became easier to speak but a great deal harder to master.

5.2 Suppletion

The type of irregularity where one word uses two roots is known as 'suppletion'. There are several outstanding instances of this in English. Comparative and superlative of *good* are *better* and *best*, in place of regular forms *good-er* and *good-est*. *Bad* has *worse* and *worst* rather than *bad-er* and *bad-est*. And the past tense of *go* is *went*, where *go-ed* would be expected.

The suppletive set *good* and *better/best* was there in Old English, and indeed in earlier stages. (Several other European languages show suppletive forms for an adjective with corresponding meaning.) In Old English, the antonym of *gōd* 'good' was *yfel* 'bad, wicked, evil'. This had suppletive comparative and superlative forms *wyrse* and *wyrst*, which have developed into modern *worse* and *worst*. The word *bad* came into Middle English (in circumstances which are not understood) and was adopted as the antonym of *good*, with *yfel > evil* being restricted to its present-day meaning. The suppletive forms *worse* and *worst* were then transferred to *bad*.

In Old English, verb *gān* 'go' had a suppletive past form *ēode*. There was also a verb *wend* 'turn' with past tense *went* (on the same pattern as *send/sent*). Around 1500, *ēode* dropped out of use. A regular past form *ga-ed* came into use in some northern dialects. But elsewhere—and soon everywhere—a new suppletive past was adopted for *go*; this was *went*, the erstwhile past of *wend*. As for *wend*, it now took on a regular past tense form *wend-ed*.

Fascinating as some of these suppletions are (a further one is the copula verb, *be*), they belong with the irregularities discussed in the previous section—most definitely *not needed* for the efficient functioning of a language. There is, however, another variety of suppletion, which cannot be dismissed so lightly.

Kyaka Enga, a language from the Highlands of Papua New Guinea, has suppletive forms for the verb 'give'. *Mailyu* is used for a 3rd person recipient and *jilyu* for 1st and 2nd person. For example (note that 3rd person can be left unstated):

Namba-me_A   suwua_O   mailyu
1sg-ERGATIVE dog   give.to.3rd.person
'I give him/her a dog'

Suwua_O   namba   jilyu
dog   1sg   give.to.1st/2nd.person
'He/she gives me a dog'

This is redundant, effectively saying something twice. But, as mentioned earlier, languages require a certain amount of redundancy to be able to function effectively in conditions that are not always ideal. If a hearer does not catch the noun phrase identifying recipient, the choice of verb form narrows this down. It is useful for important information, such as this, to be provided twice.

The value of this kind of suppletion, for 'give', is shown by its recurring in a fair number of languages, scattered across the Caucasus, India, Siberia, Meso-America, Africa, New Guinea, and no doubt more besides. Whereas many other irregularities are definitely not needed, this one—which carries meaning—is advantageous.

5.3   Grammatical redundancy

Languages sometimes repeat a particular bit of information several times. Consider the following noun phrases in Portuguese:

A menin-a nov-a alt-a bonit-a   'the beautiful tall young girl'
O menin-o nov-o alt-o bonit-o   'the beautiful tall young boy'
The child- young- tall- beautiful-

The first noun phrase includes four instances of feminine gender suffix -a (on the noun and on each of the three adjectives) plus the feminine singular form, *a*, of the definite article. The second noun phrase substitutes masculine suffix *-o* and article *o* for feminine *-a* and *a*.

Is this repetition really needed? One should first place these examples in context. In fact, only a minority of nouns in Portuguese have feminine/masculine forms similar to *menin-a/menin-o*. And there are many adjectives which have an invariant form covering both genders. Also, it is unusual for a noun phrase to include as many as three adjectival modifiers.

Surely it would be sufficient for gender to be shown just once in a noun phrase, by the initial article. What is gained by repeating it, especially since this is done inconsistently, with not all nouns and adjectives having gender-sensitive forms? A partial response could be that if one uses *bonita* alone, the final *-a* indicates reference to a beautiful female. However, this is a piecemeal business; for other adjectives—such as *inteligents* 'intelligent'—the form gives no information as to gender.

The rich set of genders in Swahili was mentioned in section 4.1. Each noun shows a prefix which combines information on gender and on number (singular versus plural), this being repeated on all modifiers within the noun phrase, and also on the verb. Noun *-kombe* 'cup' is in the general inanimate gender, shown by prefixes *ki-* for singular and *vi-* for plural:

Ki-kombe	ki-dogo	ki-moja	ki-mevunjika
ki-cup	ki-small	ki-one	ki-broken

'One small cup is broken'

Vi-kombe	vi-dogo	vi-wili	vi-mevunjika
vi-cup	vi-small	vi-two	vi-broken

'Two small cups are broken'

Such a multiplicity of agreement is not really needed. Except that it helps define the character—one might say the beauty—of Swahili. And of course the same could be said for Portuguese.

As explained in section 3.4, a case marker indicates the function of an argument (typically a noun phrase) in its clause. Some languages have nominative, used for transitive subject (A) and intransitive subject (S) functions, and accusative, for transitive object (O). Others have absolutive, for S and O, and ergative, for A.

A case marker indicates the function of the whole noun phrase. Most economically, it is added to just one word of the phrase. It can be on the head word, or the first word, or—most often—on the last word. This can be illustrated for Kugu-Nganhcara, spoken in the Cape York Peninsula of Australia. 'The two big men', in A function, is:

[pama   yoko   kuce]-ng
man   big   two-ERGATIVE

The ergative suffix marks that the noun phrase is in A function, and it is stated just once, at the end of the phrase. A quite different situation prevails a few hundred kilometres to the south-east, in Dyirbal. Here, each word in a noun phrase takes ergative suffix (which is -*nggu* after a disyllabic word ending in a vowel, and -*gu* after a trisyllabic one):

[yara-nggu   jugi-nggu   bulayi-gu]
man-ERGATIVE big-ERGATIVE two-ERGATIVE

Such multiple marking of case is plainly unnecessary. But it does have a silver lining. In Kugu-Nganhcara, the words making up a noun phrase must remain together. In Dyirbal they can be—and are—scattered at will throughout the sentence. One can tell from the shared case ending that they do make up one noun phrase.

Under (b) in section 3.4, there was description (and exemplification) of how the argument under focus in a polar question for Dyirbal is placed in sentence-initial position and marked with interrogative suffix -*ma*. Having multiple case marking, and thus freedom of word ordering, allows any word to fulfil this role.

In summary, multiple marking of a grammatical element is not economical—in some instances it could be described as downright extravagant—but it can have desirable side-effects and is not uniformly to be deplored.

5.4 Semantic redundancy

Sometimes the same meaning contrasts are coded both in grammar and in lexicon, which at first blush appears unnecessary.

Dyirbal is spoken in hilly, well-watered country between the Great Dividing Range and the Coral Sea. It has the following system of affixes:

-bayji	'short distance downhill'	-dayi	'short distance uphill'
-bayja	'medium distance downhill'	-daya	'medium distance uphill'
-bayju	'long distance downhill'	-dayu	'long distance uphill'
-balbala	'medium distance downriver'	-dawala	'medium distance upriver'
-balbulu	'long distance downriver'	-dawulu	'long distance upriver'
-guya 'across the river'			
-bawal 'long way (in any direction)'			

These may be added to any of a set of locational adverbs, such as *yalu* 'to a place here', as in:

Yalu-dawulu	nganas	banagay-gu
TO.PLACE.HERE-LONG.WAY.UPRIVER	we	go.back-PURPOSIVE

'We should go back to a place a long way upriver here (where black walnuts will now be ripe and ready to be harvested)'

Note that the twelve suffixes may also be added to 'articles', described in section 4.2.

So far, so good. But what seems surprising is that Dyirbal also has a set of verbs specifying movement up or down hill or river, or across a river:

bunga-	'go downhill'	wayñji-	'go uphill'
dada-	'go downriver'	wandi-	'go upriver'
mabi-	'cross river'		

Moreover, there are quite a few instances of one of these lexical verbs occurring with a grammatical suffix which has a corresponding meaning. For example, verb *wayñji-* 'go uphill' is used side-by-side with suffix *-dayi* 'short distance uphill' in:

Nganas	yalu-dayi	wayñji-li
we	TO.PLACE.HERE-SHORT.WAY.UPHILL	go.uphill-PURPOSIVE

'We should go to a place a short distance uphill here'

In another story, verb *wandi-* 'go upriver' co-occurs with suffix *-dawulu* 'long way upriver':

Yalu-dawulu   ngana   wandi-n
TO.PLACE.HERE-LONG.WAY.UPRIVER   we   go.upriver-PAST
'We went to a place a long distance upriver here'

And in a further narrative, verb *mabi-li* 'cross river' is accompanied by grammatical element *-guya* 'across the river':

Ngana$_S$ yalu-guya   mabi-li
we   TO.PLACE.HERE-ACROSS.RIVER   cross.river-PURPOSIVE
'We should go to a place across the river here'

Surely this duplication across grammar and lexicon is unnecessary. Why couldn't speakers just use verb *yanu-* 'go' in the last three sentences, in place of *wayñji-*, *wandi-*, and *mabi-*? All the locational information conveyed by these verbs is there already, indicated by the grammatical suffixes,

However, closer examination shows there is not absolute redundancy. This may be seen in:

Bangum   ngana$_S$ manma-ñu   bunga-n
THEN   we   shift.camp-PAST   go.downhill-PAST
    yalu-balbulu
    TO.PLACE.HERE-LONG.WAY DOWNRIVER
'Then we shifted camp, went downhill to a place a long way
    downriver'

How can it be that the verb describes going downhill, and the affix to a place downriver? Things are really quite straightforward. Rather than following the meandering course of the river, they cut across and went directly downhill to the place a long way downriver where the new camp was to be established.

This overlap between grammar and lexicon can be of some use, in a territory with a profusion of rivers and steep hills.

5.5 Repetition or no repetition

We now turn from grammar to style, describing how multiple repetition is a powerful tool of a certain spoken register, and how a proscription on repetition can be imposed when writing. The former is surely admirable, while the value of the latter is open to debate.

One of the roles of language given in section 1.1 was 'as a conduit for proselytisation'. In English (as in many other languages), there is a mode of oratorical speech which feasts on repetition.

A magnificent example occurs in Martin Luther King Jr.'s address at the Lincoln Memorial in Washington DC on 28 August 1963. After fourteen introductory paragraphs, he introduces the motif:

And so, even though we face the difficulties of today and tomorrow, I still have a dream. It is a dream deeply rooted in the American dream.

There follow eight short paragraphs, each beginning with *I have a dream*, the first one being:

I have a dream that one day this nation will rise up and live out the true meanings of its creed: 'we hold these truths to be self-evident, that all men are created equal'.

The power of Martin Luther King Jr.'s oratory is crystallised in this repetition. Indeed, it is known as 'the *I have a dream* speech'.

On a more mundane level, the same technique is employed by every breed of politician. For example:

This I promise you: there will be no new taxes
This I promise you: there will be more teachers in our schools
This I promise you: there will be shorter waiting times for surgery
And this I promise you: there will be an enhanced defence force
which can handle any emergency

Repetition is an accepted and effective device when people's ears are being targeted. However, eyes are a different matter altogether. When composing formal prose in English (and in a number of other languages), it is considered 'bad style' to repeat a lexeme (such as *promise* in the speech just quoted) or a construction type (*there will be...*). Semi-synonyms are sought. Thus, a written version of the *This I promise you* speech could be:

If elected, we undertake that no new taxes will be imposed. The party pledges that teacher numbers will be increased. We will ensure that waiting times for surgery are reduced. And, taking cognisance of the hostile world in which we all now live, we promise to up-grade our armed forces so that they are ready to respond swiftly to whatever situation may arise.

The verb *promise* is now used just once, its first three instances having been replaced by *undertake*, *pledge*, and *ensure*. In the speech, each sentence began with *I*, now replaced by *we*, *this party*, *we*, and—quite a way further on—another *we*. And each *there will be* has been rephrased.

Next, consider the first attempt by a down-to-earth scholar to write an assessment in a straightforward manner:

In his initial classification of Epicurean languages, James Jason used criteria which were unsound, and used data which were not all reliable. In the revised classification of these extinct languages, James Jason did use more scientific criteria and only used data which were accepted as reliable.

It can be seen that the verb *use* appears four times, and that there are two appearances of each of *classification, languages, James Jason, criteria, data*, and *reliable*. This is most definitely not good style. So the author settles down to eliminate repetitions:

In his initial classification of Epicurean languages, James Jason ~~used~~ employed criteria which were unsound, and used data which were not all reliable. In the revised ~~classification~~ categorisation of these extinct ~~languages~~ tongues, ~~James~~ Dr Jason did ~~use more scientific criteria~~ apply principles which are more scientific, and only ~~used data~~ referred to information which ~~were~~ was accepted as ~~reliable~~ dependable.

The revised paragraph now reads:

In his initial classification of Epicurean languages, James Jason employed criteria which were unsound, and used data which were not all reliable. In the revised categorisation of these extinct tongues, Dr Jason did apply principles which are more scientific, and only referred to information which was accepted as dependable.

This is now in felicitous style. But does it fulfil the role of communication any better? Surely not. *Use* is a high-frequency verb; why shouldn't one ~~use~~ employ it four times in one paragraph? *Categorisation* has a rather different import from *classification*. And *principles* does not have exactly the same meaning range as *criteria*. In terms of semantic content, absolutely nothing is gained by this re-phrasing, and there is a real chance of some coherence being lost.

All in all, the avoidance of repetition in modern English prose is an affectation, something which is not needed for the language to function efficiently. It doubtless conveys aesthetic grace to some people, but to others it is just a beastly nuisance. And it does depend on a goodly stock of semi-synonyms, a topic which will be addressed in section 7.3.

Chapter 6
How about complexity?

As noted in chapter 1, every present-day language has a pretty complicated grammar, many times more complex than that of our putative primitive language. Does this imply that the best languages are those furthest removed—in terms of complexity—from the primitive one? Is it the case that: 'the more complex the better'? Most certainly not. A language may satisfy many of the requirements we identify as relevant for an 'ideal' language (see chapter 10) either in a straightforward way, or in a convoluted way. The former is plainly preferable.

Some modern-day languages are certainly more complex than others. When one surveys the languages for which comprehensive grammatical descriptions have been published, it is noteworthy that a high proportion of those displaying a really complicated grammar are small, local languages, with just a few hundred or perhaps a few thousand speakers. None of these had a writing system (before recent contact with missionaries and the like), putting to rest the false idea that grammatical complexity is rooted in written language.

I experienced the intellectual delight of working—between 1991 and 2003—on the intricacies of Jarawara, spoken deep in the rainforest of southern Amazonia. Jarawara has as

125

Are Some Languages Better than Others? First Edition. R. M. W. Dixon.
© R. M. W. Dixon 2016. Published 2016 by Oxford University Press.

complicated a grammar as could be imagined. The next two sections provide a small sample of this, just to demonstrate what grammatical complication can be like.

Whereas I have, elsewhere in this book, tried to present information in a straightforward, user-friendly fashion, sections 6.1, 'Distinguishing suffixes', and 6.2, 'Multiple auxiliaries', are far more demanding. Many readers may prefer to skip these discussions, and take up the story again in section 6.3.

One intriguing feature in Jarawara grammar was presented in section 5.1, the irregular gender forms of inalienably possessed nouns whereby, for instance, 'face' is feminine *noki* and masculine *noko* (distinguished by the second vowel), while 'foot' is feminine *tame* and masculine *teme* (distinguished by the first vowel). We can now look at two more (out of very many) areas of complexity.

6.1 Distinguishing suffixes

There is a great deal of homonymy between suffixes in Jarawara. It was mentioned in section 3.2 that the only negator in this language is verbal suffix *-ra*. But *-ra* is also one variant of the feminine (f) form of immediate past (IP) tense in eyewitness (e) evidentiality (altogether, IPef). Moreover, the two *-ra*'s may occur in sequence:

(1) Faha$_S$ kowi-ra-ra-ke
     water(fem)   be.deep-NEGATOR-IPef-DECLARATIVE.f
     'The water was not deep (I saw it)'

It is reasonable to enquire how one knows which of the two *-ra* suffixes is the negator and which the tense. Well, if one alters tense-evidentiality, it is the second suffix which changes. For example, if we use the feminine form (agreeing in gender with the subject, *faha* 'water') of immediate past tense in non-eyewitness (n) evidentiality (IPnf), *-ni*, the sentence becomes:

(2) Faha_s   kowi-ra-ni-ke
     water(fem)   be.deep-NEGATOR-IPnf-DECLARATIVE.f
     'The water was not deep (I didn't see it myself)'

This shows that the negator, *-ra*, is in the first suffix slot after the verb.

One might sensibly ask: what if there were only a single *-ra* in sentence (1), how could we tell if it was the negator or immediate past tense? The answer is simple—there could not be just one *-ra* in this sentence.

To explain this, the structure of a verbal predicate should be outlined (in somewhat simplified form):

A prefixes (bound subject pronouns; causative; applicative)
B verb root
C auxiliary (AUXa), if the verb does not itself take affixes
D miscellaneous suffixes (including negator *-ra*)
E tense/evidentiality and modality suffixes
F mood suffixes (declarative, imperative, interrogative)
G post-mood suffixes (including negator *-ra*)

It should be noted that all suffixes (everything in slots D, E, F, and G) are optional. Each suffix in E, F, and G has distinct feminine and masculine forms. Items in slots B, C, and D only have this if they are word-final (that is, if there is nothing following them within the predicate).

There are two positions for the negator, slots D and G. Which one it goes into is determined by what other suffixes are chosen, according to the following rules:

(i) If there is a tense-evidentiality or modality suffix (slot E), then the negator goes into slot D, as in examples (1) and (2).

(ii) If there is no tense-evidentiality or modality suffix but there is a mood suffix (slot F), then the negator goes into slot G.

(iii) If there is neither a tense-evidentiality or modality suffix nor a mood suffix, then the negator goes into slot D.

Tense-evidentiality suffixes have a long form, which reduces. For example:

Immediate past in eyewitness evidentiality has feminine form *-hara* and masculine *-hare*.

The initial *-ha-* of these suffixes is dropped when it is an even-numbered (second, fourth, sixth, etc.) syllable from the beginning of the word. Thus, the underlying structure of the verb in (1) is *kowi-ra-hara-ke*. The *-ha-* of IPef *-hara* is the fourth syllable and is thus omitted, giving *kowi-ra-ra-ke* in (1).

If there were no negator, we would get, instead of (1):

(3) Faha$_S$ kowi-hara-ke
water(fem)   be.deep-IPef-DECLARATIVE.f
'The water was deep (I saw it)'

The *-ha-* of *-hara* is now in the third syllable, and does not drop.

Returning now to placement of the negator, if the tense suffix were omitted from (1) but mood retained then, by rule (ii), the negator goes into slot G. It is now word-final and is marked for gender: *-re* for feminine, as here, or *-ra* for masculine:

(4) Faha_s   kowi-ke-re

     water(fem)   be.deep-DECLARATIVE.f-NEGATOR.f

     'The water is not deep'

If there were no tense-evidentiality nor mood suffix then, by rule (iii), the negator goes into slot D. It is again word-final and marked for gender. But in this slot, the negator has feminine form *-ra*, as in (5), and masculine *-re*:

(5) Faha_s   kowi-ra

     water(fem)   be.deep-NEGATOR.f

     'The water is not deep'

Why on earth, one might justifiably ask, are the feminine/ masculine forms of the negator reversed between slots D and G? This relates to a general property of the predicate, which divides into two 'areas'. These are (slightly simplified):

area I	area II
items in slots B, C, and D, plus past eyewitness suffixes in slot E	past non-eyewitness and modality suffixes in slot E, plus everything in slots F and G
vowel for feminine form is lower (pronounced with the tongue lower in the mouth) than that for masculine	vowel for feminine form is higher than that for masculine
examples of feminine/masculine forms: negator (slot D) *-ra/-re*; immediate past eyewitness (slot E) *-hara/-hare*	examples of feminine/masculine forms: declarative (slot F): *-ke/-ka*; negator (slot G) *-re/-ra*

I have no explanation for the existence of these 'areas'. It's just the way the language is.

The following sentences exemplify the negator in slot D. Feminine *-ra* agrees in gender with the feminine argument in A (transitive subject) function in (6). And masculine *-re* is used for masculine (m) agreement in (7).

(6) [Mee   ati]$_O$ Jane$_A$ wato-ra
    THEY   voice   name(f)   understand-NEGATOR.f
    'Jane (a woman) can't understand what they are saying (lit. their voices)'

(7) [Mee   ati]$_O$ Okomobi$_A$ wato-re
    THEY   voice   name(m)   understand-NEGATOR.m
    'Okomobi (a man) can't understand what they are saying'

The next two sentences illustrate what happens when the declarative suffix (DEC) is included. The negator is then in slot G, with gender marking on final vowels reversed:

(8) [Mee   ati]$_O$ Jane$_A$ wato-ke-re
    THEY   voice   name(f)   understand-DEC.f-NEGATOR.f
    'Jane (a woman) can't understand what they are saying'

(9) [Mee   ati]$_O$ Okomobi$_A$ wato-ka-ra
    THEY   voice   name(m)   understand-DEC.m-NEGATOR.m
    'Okomobi (a man) can't understand what they are saying'

It appears to be a matter of style whether or not a declarative suffix is included.

We can now briefly examine another unusual feature of Jarawara grammar, the occurrence of several auxiliaries in the predicate.

6.2   Multiple auxiliaries

Of the 700 or so verbs I have recorded for Jarawara, around one-third are 'inflecting', with prefixes and suffixes being added directly to the verb root. Inflecting verbs include -kowi- 'be deep' in (1–5), -wato- 'know, understand' in (6–9), and -tafa- 'eat' in:

(10)   Jane_s   tafa-hara-ke
      name(f)   eat-IPef-DECLARATIVE.f
      'Jane just ate'

The remaining verbs are 'non-inflecting'. That is, they do not themselves accept any affixes, but are followed by an 'auxiliary' to which prefixes and suffixes are added. The great majority of non-inflecting verbs take auxiliary -na-. (This is the first type of auxiliary, and is glossed AUXa.) For example, *jaka -na-* 'walk', as in:

(11)   Jane_s   jaka   na-ra-ke
      name(f)   walk   AUXa-IPef-DECLARATIVE.f
      'Jane just walked'

In (11), the initial -ha- of the Immediate Past eyewitness feminine suffix -hara is omitted since it would be in the second syllable of the word.

About a dozen non-inflecting verbs take a different auxiliary, -*ha*-. For example *tai* -*ha*- 'go in front, be ahead', as in:

(12) Botenawaa_s   tai   to-ha-hare-ka
      name(m)   go.in.front   AWAY-AUXa-IPem-DEC.m
      'Botenawaa went in front just now'

Jarawara has several different methods of verbal 'reduplication' (see feature 7 in section 10.1); that is, repeating all or part of a verb root before or after it. In each instance, a reduplication auxiliary (glossed as AUXb) is included, and takes some or all of the verbal affixes. For certain kinds of reduplication, AUXb is -*na*-, for others it is -*ha*-. We can start with a straightforward sentence, using transitive inflecting verb -*mita*- 'hear, listen':

(13) Ati_O   ti-mita-hi!
      voice(f)   2sgA-listen-Immediate.Positive.IMPERATIVE.f
      'You listen to the voices (here and now)!'

Reduplication of the initial consonant-plus-vowel (CV) of a verb, plus reduplication auxiliary -*na*-, carries the meaning 'do a bit'. Applying this to (13), we get:

(14) Ati_O   mi-mita   ti-na-hi!
      voice(f)   REDUP-listen   2sgA-AUXb-Imm.Positive.IMPERATIVE.f
      'You listen a bit to the voices (here and now)!'

Second person singular subject prefix *ti*- and Immediate Positive Imperative suffix -*hi*, which were attached to the inflecting verb -*mita*- in (13), have now been transferred to the reduplication auxiliary (AUXb) -*na*-. Note that in Jarawara all pronouns (irrespective of their actual reference) are classed as feminine. Hence—in (13) and (14)—the feminine form, -hi-, of the imperative suffix, agrees with the 2sg subject pronominal prefix ti-.

A straightforward sentence with the non-inflecting intransitive verb wee -na- 'shine' is:

(15) Ratena$_S$ wee   to-na-ke
     lantern (f)   shine   AWAY-AUXa-DEC.f
     'The lantern is shining out'

Applying initial CV reduplication, we get:

(16) Ratena$_S$ we-wee   to-na   na-ke
     lantern (f)   REDUP-shine   AWAY-AUXa   AUXb-DEC.f
     'The lantern is blinking out (literally, shining a bit)'

There are here two auxiliaries, both -na-: AUXa belongs with the non-inflecting verb and retains prefix to- 'away', while the reduplication auxiliary, AUXb, purloins the declarative suffix -ke.

There are several kinds of verbal suffixes in Jarawara. All those in predicate slots E (tense-evidentiality and modality), F (mood), and G (post-mood) are what we can call 'normal' suffixes. That is, they are added directly onto an immediately preceding inflecting verb, auxiliary, or suffix, and later suffixes are added directly after them.

Of the miscellaneous suffixes in slot D, about half are normal (including negator -ra). For twenty-two of the remainder, no later suffix can be added directly to them. A following auxiliary is required, AUXc—which is -na- in some instances and -ha- in others—with following suffixes being attached to this. They are referred to as 'auxiliary-taking' suffixes.

And six miscellaneous suffixes are 'auxiliary-bound'. They cannot be added directly to what precedes them in the predicate but only to an auxiliary of their own, AUXd (which is always -na-). There is one suffix which is both auxiliary-taking and auxiliary-bound.

All this is fairly mind-boggling at first, but becomes clearer when exemplified. We can start with normal suffixes. Sentence (17) attaches two normal miscellaneous suffixes to inflecting verb -amosa- be 'good'; they are -misa 'up' and -waha 'now'. They are followed by the masculine form of the declarative suffix, -ka, indicating that the child being referred to is male.

(17) Inamatewe$_S$ amosa-misa-waha-ka
      child   be.good-UP-NOW-DEC.m
      'The boy is getting better now'

Sentence (18) illustrates normal miscellaneous suffix -mina 'in the morning' added to the AUXa, -na-, of non-inflecting verb jati -na- 'be alive', and followed by tense and mood suffixes.

(18) Inamatewe$_S$ jati   na-mina-ra-ke
      child   be.alive   AUXa-MORNING-IPef-DEC.f
      'The girl was (still) alive this morning' (but died later in the day)

Auxiliary-taking suffixes include -mii -na- 'walking around', -rama -na- 'unusual, unexpected', -nati -ha- 'be the only person doing something', and -kanikima -na- 'be scattered'. Each is accompanied by an AUXc, to which later suffixes within the predicate are added. This can be illustrated with -kanikima -na-, added in (19) to the inflecting verb -tafa- 'eat', and in (20) to the AUXa, -na- of the non-inflecting verb *soo* -na- 'lie (with a plural S argument)' (after earlier miscellaneous suffix -re 'on a raised surface').

(19) Mee$_S$ tafa-kanikima   na-ra-ke
     THEY   eat-SCATTERED   AUXc-IPef-DEC.f
     'They (arrived and spread out and) each ate in a different house'

(20) Tisera$_S$ soo   na-re-kanikima
     cup(f)   lie(plS)   AUXa-RAISED.SURFACE-SCATTERED
     na-ra-ke
     AUXc-IPef-DEC.f
     'The cups (for tapping rubber) were scattered across the floor (a raised surface)'

In each of these sentences, tense and mood suffixes are added to the AUXc, -na-, required by -kanikima; they cannot be added directly to -kanikima.

Auxiliary-bound suffixes have following suffixes added directly to them, but they themselves may only be added to a preceding AUXd (always -na-) supplied by them. They include -haba- 'do/happen all night', -kawaha- 'do for a while' and -wahare- 'do many times, in many places'. In (21), -wahare- is used with inflecting verb -tafa- 'eat':

(21) Okomobi$_S$ tafa   na-wahare-hare-ka
     name(m)   eat   AUXd-MULTIPLE-IPem-DEC.m
     'Okomobi ate many times in many houses'

In (22), -*wahare*- is used with non-inflecting verb *tai* -*ha*- 'go in front'. This has an AUXa, -*ha*-, but -*wahare* may not be added to it. Instead, it attaches to its own AUXd, -*na*-.

(22) Botenawaa$_S$ tai   to-ha   na-wahare-ka
      name(m)   go.in.front   AWAY-AUXa   AUXd-MULTIPLE-DEC.m
      'Botenawaa takes the lead many times'

There is just one miscellaneous suffix, -*wi* -*na*- 'continuously', which combines the unusual properties of -*kanikima* -*na*- (with respect to what follows) and of -*wahare* (with respect to what precedes). In (23), the intransitive non-inflecting verb *haa-haa* -*na*- 'laugh' has been made transitive by the addition of applicative prefix *ka*-, giving *haahaa ka-na*- 'laugh at'. This is used with suffix -*wi* -*na*- in:

(23) Jara$_A$ owa$_O$ haahaa   ka-na
      white.man(m)   ME   laugh   APPLICATIVE-AUXa
      na-wi   na-re-ka
      AUXd-CONTINUOUS   AUXc-IPem-DEC.m
      'The white man laughed at me for a considerable time'

It can be seen that -*wi* is not added to the verbal auxiliary (AUXa) but instead requires its own auxiliary (AUXd) to which it is attached. In addition, it does not permit a following suffix to be added to it, but instead requires a following auxiliary (AUXc) -*na*-, to which tense-modal and mood suffixes (-*re* and -*ka*) are attached. In all, the predicate in (23) includes three distinct tokens of the auxiliary -*na*-.

The full corpus of Jarawara includes a fair number of sentences with three auxiliaries (but none with all four). They occur in the following order: AUXa (from a non-inflecting verb), then AUXd (from an auxiliary-bound suffix), then AUXb (from reduplication), then AUXc (from an auxiliary-taking suffix).

Speakers of Jarawara experience no difficulty with this intricate organisation of auxiliaries. It is a grammatical masterpiece, an aesthetic delight. For me, working out such an outrageous system (only the bare bones of which have been sketched here) was an intellectual challenge of the most exciting and satisfying kind. But for the purpose of straightforward communication, it is rather excessive.

In order not to unduly complicate the exposition, all of the examples just quoted—except for (13) and (14)—had 3rd person subject. 1sg and 2sg subject are shown by prefixes which go onto an inflecting verb and onto the AUXa of a non-inflecting verb. Under reduplication, they are transferred to the reduplication auxiliary, AUXb. They are sometimes included on AUXc and AUXd (according to specific rules). Consider the following sentence, with three auxiliaries:

(24) Ta-tai   to-ha   na-wahare
      REDUP-go.in.front   AWAY-AUXa   AUXd-MULTIPLE
      o-ha-hamaro   o-ke
      1sgS-AUXb-FAR.PASTef   1sg-DEC.f
      'I used to go in front many times'

Non-inflecting verb *tai -ha-* (AUXa) 'go in front, be ahead' here undergoes a type of reduplication which involves repetition of the initial CV of the root plus *-ha-* as the reduplication auxiliary (AUXb); the meaning is 'do habitually'. Sentence (24) also involves auxiliary-bound suffix *-wahare* 'do many times, in many places', this being added to its own auxiliary, AUXd. The 1sg pronominal prefix, *o-*, goes on the reduplication auxiliary, AUXb. And *o-* is repeated before declarative suffix *-ke*, the two (prefix plus suffix) forming a separate word.

This is but a slender sample of the complexities in Jarawara grammar.

6.3 Losing and gaining complexity

Having had a peek into complexity, it is now time to resume the main narrative. Consider the world's major languages, each of which is used as lingua franca across a varied range of ethnic groups. They are, by-and-large, relatively low on complexity. Mandarin has a more straightforward grammar than other major Chinese languages (so-called 'dialects'). English has less complex word structure than other Germanic languages. Swahili—spoken as first or second language by well over a hundred million people in East Africa—is one of the few Bantu languages to have lost tones.

Arabic has a pretty intricate grammar, but modern Arabic languages have shed some of the complexity of the classical tongue (in which the Koran was written). As the number of people using English, world-wide, has been increasing over the past couple of centuries, so are irregularities being gradually smoothed out. Archaic forms of verbs such as *burnt, besought, learnt, wove/woven,* and *dreamt* are being replaced by regular past tense forms *burn-ed, beseech-ed, learn-ed, weav-ed,* and *dream-ed.*

A language spoken over a homogeneous terrain, by just one or two ethnic groups with similar social and mental attitudes, has more scope for special grammatical parameters than a more widely spoken language. Grammatical specification for 'up' versus 'down' was illustrated for Hua at the beginning of chapter 2, and for Dyirbal (here indicating whether with respect to hill or to river) in section 5.4. These languages are spoken in mountainous country. An 'up/down' grammatical contrast would not be found in a language spoken on plains, or in a language—such as English or Spanish—spoken by many millions of people inhabiting every type of terrain,

The set of five evidentiality specifications in Tariana was illustrated in section 4.4. There is obligatory specification of how the information coded in a statement was obtained—whether by seeing, hearing, inferring, assuming, or being told. Large evidentiality systems are found exclusively in the languages of small groups with a shared mental outlook, which correlates with having an obligatory system of this type in the grammar. In such societies, one is expected to be specific as to how something is known. To be vague is to be stupid. And specificity can also be life-preserving. Amazonian people typically attribute a human cause to each event. Saying exactly what one did and what one knew will reduce the chance of being accused of—direct or supernatural—responsibility for a death.

In essence, the grammars of major languages are unlikely to include a sophisticated evidentiality system, or specification of 'up/down'. They also tend to have simple versions of universal categories such as 'number'. Early stages of Indo-European languages had a {singular, dual, plural} system but 'dual' was lost in most branches as the language communities expanded in scope. The eminent linguist Antoine Meillet saw the loss as 'not surprising since the disappearance of the dual is a development of civilisation'. He maintained that the language of a civilised people didn't require such an unnecessary feature as dual number. He also viewed the loss of case marking as a civilising improvement. Meillet's views are odd. Dual number and case marking are most definitely aids to communication; why should 'civilised' peoples be denied them?

As a language expands its base, new speakers may acquire it a trifle imperfectly and this can lead to some overall loss in complexity. The present population of Brazil is descended from Portuguese invaders (predominantly male), the local indigenous population, and slaves brought in from Africa. There were many mixed marriages, with people acquiring Portuguese at an adult age. This explains why, in a number of respects, Brazilian Portuguese is less complex than its European counterpart.

One must of course always enquire: better for what purpose? Someone might argue that if one nation seeks to dominate others, it is an advantage to have a language which can be easily learnt. This is a topic to which we return in section 9.5.

Speakers of major languages tend to be monolingual. If millions of people in every direction from your home town use the same language as you, there is little need to acquire another. In contrast, a language spoken by just a small group may have a different language spoken a day's walk away in each direction. Multilingualism is then the natural state—for intergroup trade, cultural activities, marriage, and so on. Social contact means language contact which engenders linguistic change. A category particular to one language may be borrowed into another (and this can operate in both directions), leading to augmentation of the grammar.

In the Vaupés River Basin of north-west Brazil, multilingualism has become institutionalised. One must marry someone speaking another language. As the people explain it: 'Those who speak the same language as us are our brothers, and we do not marry our sisters.' Each person knows the language of their father (with which they identify), mother, wife, and perhaps various aunts and uncles. In the Vaupés Basin there are several closely related languages of the Tucanoan family, plus one language from the Arawak family, Tariana, which has a quite different structural profile.

There is strict prohibition against using words from another language; indeed, anyone who does so is ridiculed. However, in a multilingual situation, grammatical patterns may diffuse from one language into another, unbeknownst to the speakers. In this manner, Tariana has increased in structural complexity. To the Arawak grammar from its genetic inheritance, it has added a number of Tucanoan features. We can mention three.

(a) **Evidentiality**. As set out in section 4.4, Tariana follows Tucanoan languages in having a five-term evidentiality system: {seen, heard, inferred, assumed, told}. In contrast, its closest Arawak neighbour, Baniwa (spoken outside the multilingual Vaupés region), simply has a contrast between 'reported' and 'not reported'.

(b) **Bridging construction**. Tariana has taken over a Tucanoan pattern whereby the gist of one sentence is summarised at the beginning of the next, something like 'A did X. Having done X, A did Y'. A Tariana example is:

Pa-ita		nawiki	hinipuku-se	di-a-pidana
one-CLASSIFIER.HUMAN	man		garden-TO	3sg.m-go-REM.P.REP
'A man went to the garden'				

Kay	di-ni,	yuwapiku	di-hpani-pidana...
Thus	3sg.m-do	long.time	3sg.masc-work-REM.P.REP
'Having done thus, he worked for a long time...'			

Note that the tense-evidentiality suffix *-pidana* 'remote past reported' occurs on verb 'go' in the first sentence, but is not included in the bridging repetition.

(c) **Multiple verb suffixes.** Tariana has developed several dozen verbal suffixes, with meanings similar to those in Tucanoan languages. They include *-kawhi* 'do early in the morning', *-ñu* 'feel a sharp pang of pain (for example, when stepping on something)', *-liphe* 'hold on firmly', and *-yəna* 'do little-by-little', as in:

Emite_S   di-sape-yəna-ka
child   3sg.m-speak-LITTLE.BY.LITTLE-RECENT.PAST.VISUAL
'The male child was starting to talk little-by-little'

Other language contact situations are less regimented than that of the Vaupés River Basin. The extent to which the grammar of one community may affect that of a neighbour will depend on the kinds—and stability—of social relations between them (which may include war), relative sizes of communities, whether one is accorded special prestige, and attitudes to multilingualism. Also on the complexities of the languages. Suppose that language C has a rather complex grammar while its neighbour, L, has a considerably less complex one so that speakers of C find it easy to learn L, but not the other way round. Many members of the C community will attain a level of proficiency in L, which could lead to some features of L being incorporated into C (making it even more complex). But few speakers of L are likely to master C, so that the grammar of L is likely to be little affected by social contact between the communities.

Irregularities constitute one kind of (generally, unwanted) complexity. These may arise from historical changes which make words shorter or easier to pronounce, and at the same time introduce opacity into the grammar. In section 5.1 there was explanation of how the irregular forms of inalienably possessed nouns in Jarawara originated. Reconstruction of the proto-Arawá stage indicates that possessed nouns had an invariable root, adding *-ni* for feminine and *-ne* for masculine gender. A number of regular phonological changes then applied, producing the modern forms. Quoting feminine/masculine, the developments included:

	proto-Arawá		Jarawara
'face'	*noko-ni/*noko-ne	>	noki/noko
'foot'	*tama-ni/*tama-ne	>	tame/teme

Gender differences are now shown by the final vowel for 'face' and by the first vowel for 'foot'.

In English, irregular forms of verbs and nouns all developed from a regular pattern at some time in the past. For example, modern singular/plural forms *goose/geese* and *mouse/mice* came about as follows:

proto-Germanic	*gans	*gans-iz	*mūs	*mūs-iz
Old English (1)	gōs	gēs-iz	mūs	mȳs-iz
Old English (2)	gōs	gēs	mūs	mȳs
Modern English	goose	geese	mouse	mice
	/guːs/	/giːs/	/maus/	/mais/

At the reconstructed proto-Germanic stage, plural just involved the addition of *-iz* to the singular form. The *-i-* of *-iz* then engendered a mutation, whereby the preceding vowel was raised: $\bar{o} > \bar{e}$ in the plural of 'goose', and $\bar{u} > \bar{y}$ (where y is a rounded high front vowel, similar to that in French tu), for 'mouse'. Following this, the old plural suffix -iz was dropped. And regular vowel changes then produced the modern forms.

Sometimes we just cannot tell how irregular grammatical forms arose. For example, the auxiliary-taking suffixes of Jara-wara, discussed in the preceding section, which cannot be dir-ectly followed by any further suffix but take an auxiliary to which other suffixes are added. These include -mii -na- 'walking around', -$rama$ -na- 'unusual, unexpected', -$nati$ -ha- 'be the only person doing something', and -$kanikima$ -na- 'be scattered'. A typical change, cross-linguistically, is for lexical words to become grammatical affixes (what is called 'grammaticalisation'). Related languages in the close-knit Arawá family appear not to have such auxiliary-taking verbal suffixes. One searches assidu-ously for lexemes in other Arawá languages which might be cognate with (and the origin of) auxiliary-taking suffixes in Jarawara. Nothing eventuates. It is simply unclear (at the present stage of investigation) how this rather unusual type of complexity evolved. Similar conundrums remain for many other languages.

Dialects of language may gradually diverge more and more—perhaps as the speech communities move out of contact—until they are no longer mutually intelligible and constitute distinct languages. New languages are thus created, each being as com-plex as its progenitor.

There is a rather special variety of new languages: creoles, which evolve from pidgins. A 'pidgin' is a restricted code used for trade (or some other limited purpose) between two groups who do not have a language in common. It has a simple grammar and limited vocabulary, and cannot be regarded as a full language. Circumstances may arise (for example, through slavery) of a community whose only means of communication is a pidgin. Except that it rapidly becomes a pidgin no more. The vocabulary is extended, grammatical parameters and constructions established, so that it now has the characteristics of a full language, and is called a 'creole'. This happens quickly, but of course it is not instantaneous. A certain period of development is required before a creole acquires a level of complexity and sophistication similar to that of other languages. (Most creoles have reached this level.)

In 2001, linguist John McWhorter published a study entitled 'The world's simplest grammars are creole grammars'. What he is referring to are creoles which emerged from pidgin-hood rather recently and 'have not existed as natural languages for a long enough time for diachronic drift to create the weight of "ornament" that encrusts older languages'. Young creoles are—necessarily—lacking in complexity. But give them a little development time and they will become old creoles, as able as other languages to fulfil the roles set out in section 1.1.

In summary, the matter of complexity is tangential to evaluation of the relative worth of languages. Having a profusion of useful grammatical categories is plainly a good thing. But much complexity is an unwieldy relic of the past stages of a language and how over time the details have shifted. However, there are aspects of complexity in which a speaker (or a linguist) may delight, as adding a veneer of splendour over the workmanlike infrastructure of the language.

During recent years, unfortunate misinformation has been bandied around concerning Pirahã, an Amazonian language. The gossip (it is little more than that) is that Pirahã has a far simpler grammar than any other known language. Yet no comprehensive grammar has been produced to back up these claims. A number of intelligent and responsible Summer Institute of Linguistics missionary linguists have worked intensively on the language, including Arlo and Vi Heinricks (1960–7), and Keren Madora (from 1979, continuing until today). They confirm that Pirahã is most definitely *not* lacking in complexity, and that its character has been grossly misrepresented.

Chapter 7
How many words should there be?

There are many more similarities than there are differences between the varied groups of human beings, the ways they live and interact, and what they require in their languages. All people wake, eat, jump, laugh, vomit, speak, and remember. They plan social activities, acquire and cook foodstuffs, experience anger, jealousy, and shame, describe things as hot or wet or heavy, or as good.

Shared (one might say, universal) concepts can—most of the time—fairly easily be translated between languages. However things can get a little tricky when two languages differ in specificity. Language A may have a general verb 'carry', to which can be added an optional specification such as 'in the hand'. In contrast, language B lacks a general verb 'carry', having instead an array of (unanalysable) specific verbs: 'carry on the head', 'carry over the shoulder', 'carry against the belly', 'carry on the hip', 'carry in the hand', and perhaps more. In order to translate into language B a sentence from language A such as 'Father carried the consignment into the house', more information is required—*how* did he carry it?

Are Some Languages Better than Others? First Edition. R. M. W. Dixon.
© R. M. W. Dixon 2016. Published 2016 by Oxford University Press.

This lexical specificity is similar to grammatical requirements of 'what must be said', discussed in section 2.1. Recall that, in order to translate an English sentence *The child fell* into Jarawara, one must ascertain the sex of the child, and whether or not the speaker actually saw it happen. This is because, unlike English, Jarawara has grammatical systems of gender and evidentiality, from each of which a choice must be made.

Social conditions vary. In some circumstances it is good to be really specific, in others to be purposely vague. An ideal language would cater for both options. It may be useful to have specific unanalysable verbs for particular modes of carrying, but a general verb with the overarching meaning 'carry' will also come in handy.

People in large societies, speaking the world's major languages, vie with each other: *Mirror, mirror on the wall, who is the fairest one of all?* As pointed out in section 4.5 (on comparative constructions) many small ethnic groups—from various parts of the world—have a different modus vivendi. They do not compete, and as a consequence have no need for words such as 'race', 'win', 'lose', 'victor', or 'victory'. (In most such societies, marriages are 'arranged' by the parents, so that there is no courtship competition.)

In essence, each society needs words to describe how they live, and what their attitudes are. There is considerable commonality, across all peoples of the world, but also significant points of difference.

In the following sections, attention is paid to the desirability of specification (7.1), to the bothersome nature of homonymy (7.2), to the benefits of synonymy (7.3), and to the value gained from having a concept expressed through two word classes (7.4).

Section 7.5 then enquires about how many words are really needed.

7.1 Specification

Particular types of activity require their own terminology. A cotton loom weaves by intersecting the warp with the weft, using a heddle frame, controlled by dobbies. The vocabulary of a loom operator is not needed by us ordinary folk.

Camels are curious creatures and Arabic has scores of words dealing with their characteristics. There is one set of terms relating to how often a camel drinks: only every three days, or every two days, or every day, or once during the day and once at night, and so on. We also find 'a female camel who does not allow herself to be milked', 'a female camel who always leads the other camels', 'a white camel with a different coloured tail', amongst many other labels.

In his ethnographic monograph on the Nuer, from southern Sudan, E. E. Evans-Pritchard remarked: 'Linguistic profusion in particular departments of life is one of the signs by which one quickly judges the direction and strength of a people's interest... Like all the pastoral Nilotes, [the Nuer] use an enormous number of words and phrases about cattle and the tasks of herding and dairy-work.'

He notes that there are 'ten principal colour terms', which seem particularly oriented to the hues of cattle: 'white (*bor*), black (*car*), brown (*lual*), chestnut (*dol*), tawny (*yan*), mouse-grey (*lou*), bay (*thiang*), sandy-gray (*lith*), blue and strawberry roan (*yil*), and chocolate (*gwir*). When an animal is of a single colour, it is described by one of these terms.' When there is a combination of colours, special terms come into play. For example, mainly mouse-grey but with a white face, or with a white back, or with a white shoulder, or with a white belly. There are several score other terms for varied colour combinations.

Cotton-weaving, camel-using, and cattle-herding are specialised activities, particular to certain types of people. We can now examine terms with a wider distribution. For example 'queen'.

The word *queen* in English is ambiguous. If I should introduce someone as *Queen Matilda of Bilyana*, you cannot tell whether she is simply a queen-consort, the wife of the King of Bilyana, or a queen in her own right, the ruler of this small state. There is no such ambiguity in Hungarian. This language has no simple word for 'queen'. What it does is derive designations for the two varieties of queen from *király* 'king' as follows:

király + -*né* ('wife of') gives *király-né* 'queen-consort'
király + -*nő* ('feminine') gives *király-nő* 'queen-ruler'

Kinship is universal. Everyone has a mother and a father and each language has distinct labels for them. Everyone has four grandparents, but some languages—including English—do not have four distinct terms. This can cause confusion. For instance, mother says *We're going for lunch with Granny on Sunday*, and daughter enquires *Do you mean Granny Smith* [mother's mother] or *Granny Jones* [father's mother]?

There are four grandparent terms in many languages, including Dyirbal:

bulu	'father's father (and his brothers and sisters)'
babi	'father's mother (and her sisters and brothers)'
ngagi	'mother's father (and his brothers and sisters)'
gumbu	'mother's mother (and her sisters and brothers)'

In Dyirbal, each noun can be accompanied by a kind of article, which indicates gender: *balan* for female and *bayi* for male humans. Mother's mother is *balan gumbu*, and so are her sisters (note that sisters count as equivalent within the Dyirbal kinship system). Mother's mother's brother is set off as *bayi gumbu*.

In English, mother's mother and father's mother are both *grandmother* or *granny*, but at least we do have a term for them. There are other kinship categories for which no straightforward label is available.

- Suppose that I am married to Mary, my wife, and Mary has a brother, Pete, who is thus my brother-in-law. Pete marries Kate. What relation is Kate to me?
- My son, John, has a mother-in-law (his wife's mother), Vera. What relation is Vera to me?

English has no terms for the relationships of Kate and Vera to me. But languages spoken in India do have such kin categories, and Indian English has innovated appropriate labels. These include:

co-sister-in-law   'spouse's sister-in-law'
co-mother-in-law   'son's or daughter's mother-in-law'

Kate is my co-sister-in-law and Vera my co-mother in-law.

The sun and the moon are visible from all places, but not at all times. They are only rather rarely seen in the sky together. A few languages have a single word, covering these two celestial objects. For instance Tariana, from north-west Amazonia, has *keri* 'sun, moon'. Usually, the context makes it clear which sense is intended. On the rare occasions when specification is required, one says, literally, 'keri of the day' or 'keri of the night'.

We can now travel more than a thousand kilometres to the south, and examine terms in Jamamadi, Jarawara, and Banawá, three mutually intelligible dialects of a single language:

	'moon'	'sun'	'thunder'
Jamamadi	abariko	mahi	bahi
Jarawara	abariko	bahi	bahi
Banawá	abariko	mahi	mahi

Jamamadi retains the original forms; 'sun' and 'thunder' differ only in the initial consonant—bilabial nasal *m* and bilabial stop *b*. The other dialects have simply collapsed the two forms into one, but in different directions. Why the change? We don't know. However, the sense intended will generally be clear from context of use: the sun shines (and doesn't roar) whereas thunder roars (and doesn't shine).

Although some languages do get by without them, it is clearly ideal to have distinct words for 'moon' and 'sun' (and for 'thunder'). But why stop at one word for each? We find two in Nyawaygi, an Australian language:

jula	'hot sun (at midday)' (also 'summer time')
bujira	'less hot sun (as in the early morning)'
ngilgan	'full moon'
balanu	'new moon'
guñjunu	'the early stages of a thunderstorm'
migubara	'a thunderstorm in its full ferocity'

Let us now examine activities common to all people (and animals too)—eating and drinking:

<small>VERB</small>   <small>OBJECT</small>
'eat'   foodstuff
'drink'   liquids

The things which can be object for 'eat' are quite different from those which can be object for 'drink', so that a language could make do with just one verb covering both eating and drinking. Quite a few languages are like this, including Warlpiri, from Central Australia, where *nga-* is 'eat, drink (that is, consume)'. The nature of the object makes clear which sense is intended: *nga-* plus 'beer' is 'drink', while *nga-* plus 'lizard' is 'eat'.

It could work the other way round. Having separate verbs for 'eat' and 'drink', there could be one or more nouns which refer to both a solid and a liquid. Suppose that one such was *grine* 'grape, wine'. In the context 'eat grine', the noun would be understood as referring to grapes, and in 'drink grine' it must be referring to wine.

In some languages, verbs of consumption can have even wider scope. Compare Manambu and Yalaku, related languages from the small Ndu family in Papua New Guinea:

	Manambu	Yalaku
'eat'	kə-	ha-
'drink'	kə-	ha-
'smoke tobacco'	kə-	ha-
'chew betelnut'	jə-	ha-

In Manambu *kə-* is used for eating, drinking, and smoking; one can tell which activity is involved from the nature of the object.

The cognate verb *ha-* in Yalaku has had its meaning extended to also include chewing betelnut.

There are languages which have gone in the opposite direction, with several verbs for modes of eating. The Girramay dialect of Dyirbal, for instance, has three rather specific verbs of eating (all transitive), depending on the nature of the foodstuff that is being consumed (the foodstuff is the O argument):

rubimal	'eat fish'
burnyjal	'eat meat'
nanbal	'eat vegetables'

This multiplicity of eating verbs might be considered redundant, since information coded in the verb can be inferred from the type of foodstuff involved. It does, however, have a use. Each verb can be made intransitive (by adding antipassive suffix *-lnga-*), and then indicates the type of food being consumed without the need to specify exactly what it is. Compare:

TRANSITIVE	Jani-nggu$_A$	mirraño$_O$	nanba-n
	John-ERGATIVE	black.bean	eat.vegetables-PRESENT
	'John is eating black beans'		
INTRANSITIVE	Jani$_S$	nanba-lnga-ñu	
	John	eat.vegetables-ANTIPASSIVE-PRESENT	
	'John is eating vegetables'		

Jarawara also has a number of transitive verbs of eating, but these describe the nature of the action, not the type of object involved. We find:

-kaba-	'eat where a lot of chewing is involved (this would be used of meat, fish, sweet corn, yams, manioc, biscuits, etc.)'
jome -na-	'eat where little or no chewing is needed, e.g. eating an orange or banana (also used for swallowing a pill)'
komo -na-	'eating which involves spitting out seeds (e.g. *jifo*, the fruit of the murity palm, *Mauritia vinifera*)'
bako -na-	'eating by sucking (e.g. water melon, cashew fruit)'

For some foods, there is more than one way of eating it, shown by appropriate choice of verb. For example, eating a pineapple can be described by *jome -na-* or by *bako -na-*.

In summary, it is good to be as specific as is generally needed, to avoid ambiguity. Separate terms for 'queen-ruler' and 'queen-consort' are certainly useful, as are labels for all four grandparents, and for 'spouse's sister-in-law', 'son or daughter's mother-in-law', and the like. Most languages have distinct terms for 'sun', 'moon', and 'thunder', and also for 'eat' and 'drink'. It is possible to be economical and combine some of them. This will slightly—but only slightly—reduce the facility of communication. Or there may be further specification of 'sun', 'moon', 'thunder', or of 'eat'—a sort of luxury in which each language indulges for some areas.

7.2 Homonymy

Having two words with the same form but quite different meanings always carries the possibility of misunderstanding. However, the degree of confusion that is likely depends on the meanings of the homonyms, and their functional proclivities. We can briefly discuss four homonym pairs in English: nouns *bank*, and adjectives *funny*, *hot*, and *curious*.

(a) *bank*. The homonyms here have different genetic origins.

- *Bank₁* 'a raised or sloping area of ground, especially at the edge of a river' came into Middle English, probably from Old Norse, about 1200 CE.
- *Bank₂* 'an institution for receiving, lending, exchanging, and safe-guarding money' was a loan from Romance languages into early Modern English, around 1500. The original meaning was 'a money-dealer's table or bench'.

The two words *bank* are used in entirely different textual and situational contexts, so that there is minimal chance of confusion arising.

(b) *funny*. In his 1755 dictionary, Dr Samuel Johnson designated *fun* as 'a low cant word' and defined it as 'sport; high merriment; frolicksome delight'.

- *Funny₁* came into use about 1750 with the meaning 'amusing, provoking a smile or laughter'.
- *Funny₂* has the meaning 'strange, peculiar, puzzling' and dates from about 1800. It was originally an offshoot of *funny₁*.

The meanings are so different that these are best regarded as two lexemes. They are used in overlapping contexts, so as to cause definite confusion. When I was at primary school, in England in the 1940s, we dealt with this by enquiring: *Is it funny-ha-ha or funny-peculiar?*

(c) *hot*. This is another instance of two adjectives, with quite different meanings, evolving from the same source.

- *hot₁* 'of high temperature' goes back to Old English.
- *hot₂* 'very spicy (food), with a pungent, biting taste due to the use of chillies, peppers, etc.' developed out of *hot₁* in Middle English times, around 1200.

The fact that both words *hot* are used of food can create real difficulty. If someone says *Sorry, this dish is too hot for me*, it is unclear in which way it is unsatisfactory. An English friend has a German wife and their daughters grew up bilingual. When speaking in English about food, the girls avoid confusion by never using the English word *hot*, substituting instead *heiß* 'hot in temperature' or *scharf* 'very spicy' from German.

(d) *curious.* This was a loan from French into Middle English. Both major meanings go back a long way:

- *curious₁ (about)* 'wanting to know, inquisitive'
- *curious₂* 'unusual, surprising, difficult to understand'

The two homonyms may be used in the same context. If one hears *She's a curious child*, either *curious₁* or *curious₂* could be intended (intonation may possibly help to disambiguate). The disparate meanings are shown by the observation that someone may be curious₁ (inquisitive) about a person who is curious₂ (unusual).

French has the same two meanings for *curieux*, but employs a grammatical technique to distinguish them. For sense 1 the adjective follows its noun, and for sense 2 it precedes. For example, *un enfant curieux* 'a curious₁ child' and *un curieux enfant* 'a curious₂ child'.

Ambiguity may also arise when there are several grammatical elements with different meanings and functions but the same form. A notable exemplar of this is the English suffix -s:

> suffix written as -s; pronounced /əz/ after a sibilant, /s/ after a voiceless sound, and /z/ elsewhere
>
> (a) on a verb, indicates 3rd person singular subject in 'present tense'
> (b) on a noun, marks plural number
> (c) at the end of a noun phrase (which can be just a noun) marks possessor; then generally accompanied by an apostrophe

In section 2.6 we showed that *The Dutch study changes on a daily basis* is ambiguous, the two interpretations being:

(1) [The Dutch$_{ADJECTIVE}$ study$_{NOUN}$] change-s$_{VERB}$ on a daily basis

(2) [The Dutch$_{NOUN}$] study$_{VERB}$ change-s$_{NOUN}$ on a daily basis

Suffix -s on *change* has sense (a) in (1) and (b) in (2). The ambiguity here also relates to three lexemes undertaking double duty: *Dutch* is an adjective in (1) but a noun in (2), *study* is a noun in (1) and a verb in (2), with the reverse applying for *change*.

We do not have to invoke double duty to demonstrate possible ambiguity between the plural and possessor functions of -s. It is necessary to omit an apostrophe, which is, of course, not shown in speaking. The sentence *The vicar's wife baked a cake and the deacons baked scones* could be understood as meaning that the deacons themselves baked scones:

(3) The vicar's wife baked a cake and the deacon-s baked scones

Here the -s on *deacon* is just plural, sense (b). Alternatively, this -s on *deacon* could be sense (c) marking a possessor, effectively modifying a following noun *wife*, which can be omitted since it is the same as the head noun in the subject noun phrase of the first clause:

(4)   The vicar's wife baked a cake and the deacon's (wife) baked scones

In (4) it is not the deacon who baked scones but his wife. (The apostrophe for possessor disambiguates the written but not the spoken form. Don't forget that we speak a great deal more than we write.)

It is harder—but not impossible—to construct a sentence which is ambiguous due to -s having either sense (a) or sense (c). Consider *The circus shows acrobats care*. This may be parsed in two ways:

(5)   [The circus]$_{\text{NOUN.PHRASE}}$ show-s$_{\text{VERB}}$ acrobats$_{\text{NOUN}}$ care$_{\text{NOUN}}$ (that is, the circus looks after its acrobats)

(6)   [The circus show-'s$_{\text{NOUN-POSSESSOR}}$ acrobats]$_{\text{NOUN.PHRASE}}$ care$_{\text{VERB}}$ (that is, the acrobats belonging to the circus show care about whether they perform well)

There is again double duty, *show* functioning as a verb in (5) and as a noun in (6), and *care* the reverse. Suffix -s on *show* has sense (a) in (5) and sense (c) in (6).

New homonyms may arise, through phonological change, through social change, or through political manoeuvring.

Language-wise this can seldom be considered an advantageous step—losing a distinction is always a dubious thing.

There are two kinds of potato products which are called *french fries* and *chips* in America but *chips* and *crisps* in England. That is, *chips* has a different reference in the two countries. Australia used to be like England but marketing strategies led to *crisps* being called *chips*, as in the USA. The clumsy American term *french fries* was not adopted, leaving *chips* with double denotation:

	AMERICA	ENGLAND	AUSTRALIA
long wedges of potato, deep-fried; eaten hot with a meal	french fries	chips	chips
potato slivers, fried, cooled and packaged; eaten cold as a snack	chips	crisps	chips

This does lead to confusion.

Let us now look at another instance of a useful distinction becoming obscured. Until recently, *gender* was a technical term in grammar only very occasionally being employed to directly describe physical attributes, for which the term *sex* was preferred. In recent years, *sex* has been largely replaced by *gender*. An application form used to ask for your 'sex'; now it enquires about your 'gender'. That is:

	TRADITIONAL USAGE	CHANGED USAGE
grammatical category, two of whose terms are typically feminine and masculine	gender	gender
physical type—female or male	sex	gender

If followed through, this can lead to real difficulties for grammarians. Instead of saying *Feminine gender covers nouns referring to female sex*, one would have to say *Feminine gender covers nouns referring to female gender*. Sticking to traditional terminology I wrote, at the beginning of chapter 3: *Just as languages without gender can still indicate sex*... Conforming to modern usage, this should have been: *Just as languages without gender can still indicate gender*...,which would have been nonsensical. Alack-a-day!

Languages differ considerably in how many homonyms they include. For example, Dyirbal, in Australia, has only a handful whereas Jarawara, in Brazil, teems with them. Why should this be? One reason lies in the number of word frames available. In both languages, the great majority of roots have no more than two syllables. Dyirbal has thirteen consonants and three vowels but a complex word structure, CV(C)(C)CV(C), yielding a possible 7,425 disyllabic forms. Jarawara has eleven consonants and four vowels but a simpler word structure, (C)V(C)V. There are just over 2,000 possible forms, about one-third as many as Dyirbal. With so many fewer phonological frames to utilise, no wonder that Jarawara resorts to homonymy.

This language has many homonym sets with two members, and quite a few with more. An example involving nouns is:

jifo   'fire, firewood' (feminine gender)
jifo   'hammock' (masculine gender)
jifo   'buriti (a palm species *Mauritia vinifera*)' (masculine gender)

Jifo meaning 'fire, firewood' and *jifo* meaning 'buriti' can occur in the same environment, and the gender contrast will distinguish them. 'Hammock' and 'buriti' are both masculine but these two nouns are likely to be used in different discourse contexts.

A homonym set across word classes is:

fowa 'bitter manioc (*Manihot esculenta*)'; masculine noun
fowa 'mortar (for grinding)'; feminine noun
fowa 'swell, overflow, flood'; intransitive inflecting verb
fowa variant form of intransitive inflecting verb 'lie in water' used when there is a prefix (the form is *hofa* when there is no prefix)

The two nouns are distinguished by gender and the two verbs by what is likely to be subject. 'Lie in water' generally has an animate subject—a person or a pig—whereas 'swell, overflow, flood' is likely to have as subject a water feature or a body part (one narrative includes *O-boko fowa-ke* 'My chest swelled up').

In summary, homonyms can be a distraction to efficient communication, especially if they may appear in similar contexts. There is always need for redundancy, and this need may be increased to counteract homonymy. Also, the possibilities for ellipsis may be curtailed if there is rampant homonymy.

One way to avoid the ambiguity attached to a homonymous term is to replace it by a synonym (if there is one), which leads into the next section.

7.3 Synonymy

Homonymy is when two words with different meanings have the same form. Synonymy is when two words, with the same meaning, have different forms. Hyponymy is when the meaning of one word is included within the meaning of another. For example, specific labels *cat*, *dog*, *sheep*, and *horse* are hyponyms of the generic noun *animal*. Every cat is an animal but it is not the case that every animal is a cat.

Here are a few verb hyponym sets in English:

GENERAL TERM	HYPONYMS
give	bestow, bequeath, confer, donate
tell	narrate, relate, notify, inform
kill	murder, execute, assassinate, slaughter
laugh	chuckle, giggle, titter, chortle
throw	chuck, hurl, fling, lob

Hyponyms abound in every language, but what about synonyms? Do we ever get two words which have *exactly* the same meaning? What could be the use of this? In fact, synonymy serves varied purposes in different languages, according to the ways in which they organise their discourse.

Dyirbal exhibits a great deal of ellipsis and this motivates an avoidance of repetition in discourse. If one man asks another 'What are you going hunting for?' he is likely to receive a one-word answer, something like *barrgan-gu* ('wallaby-DATIVE') 'for wallabies'. For a polar question such as 'Are you going walk-about?' the reply could be just *nga* 'yes' or *yimba* 'no'.

We find a completely different discourse technique in Yidiñ, Dyirbal's northerly neighbour. In Yidiñ, the response to a statement or answer to a question must be a full sentence, with predicate and core arguments. If someone asks 'What are you going hunting for?', the reply might be 'I'm going hunting for wallabies' (it could not be just a single word 'for wallabies').

It is not good style in Yidiñ for the answer to employ exactly the same words as the question. To achieve this, synonyms are substituted. For example, suppose that there is a question (marked by final rising intonation):

Ñundu~S~ burrgi-ng?
2sg   go.walkabout-PRESENT
'Are you going walkabout?'

The answer to this could be:

(Yiyi)   ngayu~S~   yaji-l
yes   1sg   go.walkabout-PRESENT
'(Yes,) I am going walkabout'

The initial *yiyi* 'yes' is optional and can be omitted. The following *ngayu yaji-l* must be stated.

It can be seen that *yaji-* has been substituted in the answer for *burrgi-* in the question. These are intransitive verbs meaning 'go walkabout', and they appear to be exact synonyms. Indeed, it seems that this and other synonym pairs exist just for the purpose of felicitous discourse; that is, avoiding lexical repetition. If the question had used *yaji-* then *burrgi-* would have been appropriate in the response. As a speaker explained it to me: 'If other fellow say *yaji-l*, you tell him back *burrgi-ng*, and same thing other way 'round. That's all there is to it.'

The situation in Yidiñ is unusual, with exact synonyms existing for discourse replacement. In English, and in other languages, there are no absolutely exact synonyms. Two words may have similar meanings but they are never substitutable, one for the other, in every circumstance. Consider *try* and *attempt*. Either may be followed by: *to work hard, to climb the mountain, to win support*, and much more. But *try* could not be substituted in *He didn't even attempt a reply*, nor could *attempt* be in *Why not try the new recipe*, or *Don't try the boss's patience!* We find that *try* and *attempt* are semi-synonyms.

In section 5.5 we described how, when composing formal prose in English, it is considered 'bad style' to repeat a lexeme. Unlike in Yidiñ, there are no exact synonyms and so semi-synonyms are utilised. A couple of passages were examined in section 5.5, and the following substitutions noted:

BASIC TERMS	SEMI-SYNONYMS TO AVOID REPETITION
promise	undertake, pledge, ensure
use	employ
classification	categorisation
languages	tongues
criteria	principles
data	information
reliable	dependable

Such substitutions may make the passages more felicitous (in terms of current perceptions) but they don't always retain the same semantic nuances. As was remarked earlier, *categorisation* has a rather different import from *classification*, and *principles* does not have exactly the same meaning range as *criteria*.

English does have an awful lot of semi-synonyms. How did this come about? In essence, the more mixed a language's history is, the richer its lexicon is likely to be. After the Norman conquest, Middle English had a core vocabulary inherited from Old English (and other Germanic sources), which was augmented by a huge number of loans from French and other Romance languages. There are many pairs of Germanic and Romance words which have pretty similar meanings. They include:

GERMANIC	ROMANCE	GERMANIC	ROMANCE
answer	reply	frighten	terrify
ask	enquire	help	assist
begin	commence	need	require
bewilder	confuse	overturn	capsize
build	construct	show	demonstrate
choose	select	want	desire
find	discover	warn	caution
forgive	pardon	worry	concern

We also find semi-synonym pairs which are both of Romance origin, such as: *allow* and *permit, copy* and *imitate, envy* and *jealousy, postpone* and *defer, try* and *attempt.*

Each word has its own function, its own meaning, its own character. We often find two words which have very similar meaning, but which differ in their pragmatic import. For instance:

MILD	STRONGER
intervene	interfere
question	interrogate
request	demand
grumble	complain

A friendly intervention may be welcome, but interference is annoying. Interrogation (perhaps conducted by the secret police) sounds terrifying, while a few questions from a well-disposed journalist may be quite pleasant. A request is polite but a demand brusque. And a shop assistant doesn't mind a customer having a bit of a grumble, but when they complain to the manager things can get unpleasant.

In essence, synonyms and close semi-synonyms are a bit of a luxury, but can have important discourse, pragmatic, and other roles. An extravagance here must be weighed against indulgencies in other areas, as will be discussed in the next chapter.

7.4 Overlapping word classes

Prototypically, nouns refer to things, adjectives to properties, and verbs to actions and states. But languages expand on this in individual ways.

English is typical of large languages spoken by socially articulated communities in that it includes a considerable number of 'abstract nouns'. These are of two main varieties. The first sort names a type of property relating to a set of adjectives. For example:

ABSTRACT NOUN	ADJECTIVES
size	big, little, large, small
age	old, new, young
height	high, low, tall, short
hardness	hard, soft
colour	black, white, red, green, blue, yellow, etc.

Some of these abstract nouns are independent lexemes (*size, age, colour*) while others are derived from one of the adjectives (*height,* also *width, depth,* etc.). Suffix *-ness* can be added to many adjectives, deriving an abstract noun; besides *hard-ness* there are *round-ness, strange-ness, correct-ness,* and a goodly number more.

Abstract nouns are most useful lexemes, but most of them are not strictly necessary. Rather than asking *What size/age/height/ hardness is it?* one could perfectly adequately say *How big/old/ high/hard is it?*

An exception is *colour*. There is no satisfactory way of rephrasing *What colour is it?* Many languages which have a fair number of basic colour terms lack this abstract noun, and it is a real deficiency. One has to resort to 'What does it look like?' or something of that nature.

English is rich in abstract nouns referring to adjective-type properties. Sometimes it is the noun which provides the root, with an adjective being derived from it. For example, *delight-ful, greed-y. Jealous* is an adjective and *envy* a noun, with derivations going in both directions, creating abstract noun *jealous-y* and adjective *envi-ous*.

The other variety of abstract noun relates to actions. For example:

ABSTRACT NOUN	VERBS
journey	travel
blow	hit, strike
thought	think
admiration	admire

The abstract noun may be related in form to a verb, as with *thought*. In English there are quite a number of nominalising suffixes which apply to verbs. For example, *-(at)ion* in *admir-ation, assassin-ation, imitat-ion,* and *-ment* in *resent-ment, announce-ment, judge-ment.* In addition, many lexemes do double duty as verb and as noun; for instance, *fight, voyage, dance,* and *smile.*

Other languages undertake different extensions to the proto-typical reference. Dyirbal does not have abstract nouns—nothing like 'journey', 'admiration', 'size', 'age', or 'colour'. One simply has to use the appropriate verb or adjective.

However, Dyirbal does have considerable semantic overlap between the classes of verb and adjective. A sample of these is:

	VERB		ADJECTIVE	
(i)	ñajul	'cook'	ñamu	'cooked'
(ii)	dadil	'cover'	ngulguñ	'covered'
(iii)	gulbal	'block'	gumun	'blocked'
(iv)	bangganday	'be sick'	wulmba	'sick'

There is in fact a clear difference of meaning in each case, with the verb referring to an action, or getting into a state, or being in a state that varies with time, and the non-cognate adjective referring to either a state that is the result of an activity, or a state that is semi-permanent. There is a slightly different semantic contrast for each verb/adjective pair. Taking them one at a time:

(i) The transitive verb *ñajul* refers to the act of cooking; its participle *ñaju-ngu* can describe something being cooked a bit or a lot, not enough or too much. In contrast, the non-cognate adjective *ñamu* means 'cooked to perfection, ready to eat'.

(ii) The transitive verb *dadil* refers to any sort of act of covering; its participle *dadi-ngu* can describe a blanket over just half a sleeping person. In contrast, the adjective *ngulguñ* means 'covered in just the right manner, covered all over'.

(iii) The transitive verb *gulbal* can refer to any kind of blocking; its participle *gulba-ngu* can be used to describe a temporary obstruction across a path. In contrast, the non-cognate adjective *gumun* refers to

169

something permanently blocked; for example, a road that has been closed off for good, or a road that simply stops at a certain place, never having been constructed any further.

(iv) The intransitive verb *bangganday* is used to describe feeling sick or ill (or just weary); the participle *bangganda-ngu* refers to someone who is under the weather at present, but is expected to get better. In contrast, the adjective *wulmba* refers to someone who is truly sick and is expected to die. (Death is believed to be caused by sorcery, so that using *wulmba* of a person is saying that a sorcerer has done something to them which will result in their death.)

In summary, having more than one word class covering what is essentially a single concept adds fluidity. While not strictly necessary (except for 'colour' and perhaps a few other items), the semantic nuances can be of considerable practical use.

7.5 How many words are needed?

How many lexemes do present-day languages have? What size should a decent working vocabulary be? Neither of these is an easy question.

The online edition of the compendious *Oxford English Dictionary* currently (November 2014) shows 275,000 entries. However, this deals with the entire history of the language, not just its present state. Many entries are marked 'obsolete' or 'dialectal'. Shakespeare, in his plays, uses about 20,000 words and Milton, in his poems, only around 8,000. By extrapolating from dictionary samples, I estimate myself to have an active vocabulary (words I use) of about 21,000, adding about 2,000 more for passive vocabulary (words I would recognise but am unlikely to use).

Of course, not all words are equally common. The Cobuild dictionary states that the most frequent 1,720 words account for 75 per cent of all English usage, and the next most frequent 12,880 a further 20 per cent. That is, 14,600 words cover 95 per cent. The remaining 5 per cent of usage is made up of how many more uncommon words? Ten thousand, or twenty, or fifty?

Languages may have more—perhaps many more—words than they really need. We can enquire what might be the minimum number of words such that one is able to say anything one wants to. In the 1920s, C. K. Ogden invented 'Basic English', which used just 850 orthographic words. These included 600 nouns, 150 adjectives, and just 16 verbs. They were: *come, get, give, go, keep, let, make, put, seem, take, be, do, have, say, see, send*. There were also grammatical words such as articles, demonstratives, pronouns, interrogatives. And 22 prepositions: *about, across, after, against, among, at, before, between, by, down, from, in, off, on, over, through, to, under, up, with, for, of*.

It was all a bit of a fraud, however. English has a large number of 'phrasal verbs'. These consist of a simple verb form plus one or two prepositions, Each phrasal verb has its own meaning (which cannot be inferred from the meanings of the components) and must be considered a distinct lexeme in its own right.

There are many homonym sets among phrasal verbs. For example, we can recognise at least seven distinct verbs *make up*, plus *make up to, make up for*, and *make (it) up with*:

make up a story or poem
make up a bed for a visitor
make up a page of a newspaper
make up one's face for the camera (using make-up)
make up a medicine by mixing the ingredients

make up a four for bridge
make up one's mind
make up to the boss
make up for wasted time/past failures
make it up with someone you had fallen out with

Other phrasal verbs commencing with *make* include: *make off* 'leave in a hurry', *make off with* 'steal', *make for* 'move towards', *make (nothing) of (it)*, 'can't understand', and *make over* 'transfer'.

Basic English allowed for combinations of any of its sixteen simple verbs (which are those that feature most prominently in phrasal verbs) with any prepositions, thus generating three or four thousand additional lexemes.

How many words does a language need? How many words do most of the non-major languages actually have? All that can be offered is an educated guess—probably between five and ten thousand. English and other major languages have many more, partly through multiple semi-synonyms, but mainly due to so many particular fields of endeavour: specialised terms used in law, music, art, and all manner of trades and sciences.

Chapter 8
The limits of a language

Linguists typically throw out the aphorism: languages differ not in what one can say but in what one must say.

The first part of this proposition is open to serious doubt. Is it really the case that everything can be said in every language? Or, rephrasing the question: can everything which can be said in language A be translated—with reasonable facility—into language B?

There is a good deal of commonality between peoples of the world, but also a fair degree of particularity, which distinguishes them. This is reflected in the grammar and vocabulary of each language, which express cultural conventions and views and mirror a style of living.

Section 8.2 examines the difficulties of translating culture-specific statements between languages. Before venturing into such tricky territory, section 8.1 reviews the range of obligatory grammatical categories—what must be said—and wonders why each language does not include them all. The final section, 8.3, weighs up the factors involved in putting together a language, and in speaking it.

Are Some Languages Better than Others? First Edition. R. M. W. Dixon.
© R. M. W. Dixon 2016. Published 2016 by Oxford University Press.

The limits of a language

8.1 What must be said

Section 2.1 explained how each language has a number of grammatical systems from which a choice *must* be made if a grammatical sentence is to be produced. We surveyed the obligatory specifications needed to describe a child having fallen, in English, Dyirbal, and Jarawara:

- In English one must say whether definite (*the*) or indefinite (*a*). There is no similar grammatical category for the other two languages.
- Each count noun in English must be specified as singular (zero ending) or plural (suffix -*s*). In Jarawara just four nouns have distinct singular and plural forms. Dyirbal has no obligatory grammatical category for number marking on nouns.
- Each noun in Jarawara belongs to one of the two genders, masculine and feminine; these are marked on modifiers within the noun phrase, and on the verb. Dyirbal has a system of four genders (see section 4.1), shown on an 'article' which typically accompanies each noun. There is in English no grammatical category of gender (as the term is used here), just sex-based 3rd person singular pronouns.
- English and Dyirbal each has just one past tense. In Jarawara a choice must be made from a three-term system: immediate past (from a moment ago to a few months in the past), recent past (from a few months to a few years ago), far past (further back).
- For each statement in past tense, Jarawara requires specification as to whether or not the event described was actually seen: eyewitness versus non-eyewitness. There is no grammatical category of evidentiality in English or Dyirbal.

Chapter 3 discussed grammatical categories which are found in every language, and the various ways of dealing with them. Then chapter 4 reviewed a number of categories which occur in many—but not all—languages, and are undoubtedly most useful. Surely it would be beneficial if every language included all of these categories, each in its fullest and most explicit form. We can list some of the more important ones.

(1) **Mood** (section 3.1). The clearest situation is where there is explicit marking (for example, by an affix to the verb, not just by intonation) for the three canonical moods describing types of speech act: declarative, imperative, interrogative.

Some languages have two (or more) imperatives: do it now, or do it at some other time or place. These are undoubtedly worthwhile for languages in which they occur and presumably would be so for every language. There are always imperatives for a 2nd person subject. Some languages also have them for 1st and 3rd persons—why not all languages?

It is helpful to have, as some languages do, a number of techniques for asking polar questions—relating to whether it is an open enquiry, or if confirmation is expected, or if there is an overtone of surprise or doubt.

(2) **Negation** (3.2). Maximum clarity obtains when there is independent marking for clausal negation (not by an affix which, for instance, replaces subject markers). It is also good to be able to negate subordinate clauses (as in *I saw that John was not working*) and also clausal arguments (*No child could solve that puzzle*).

(3) **Possession** (3.3). It is desirable to show possession not just by juxtaposition of two nouns, but by an explicit grammatical marker either on the possessor (genitive) or on the possessed (pertensive). There are three basic types of possession:

whole–part (*Mary's nose*), ownership (*Kate's car*), and kinship (*Jane's father*). Many languages distinguish some or all of these—every language could profitably do so. It would also enhance clarity if something different from possessive marking could be used for relations of association, such as *John's dentist*.

(4) Identifying roles (3.4). If a clause consists of words 'John', 'Tom', and 'punched', it is necessary to know who was the puncher and who the punchee. This can be shown by bound pronouns (to some extent), or by word order (as in English), or by case marking on each noun phrase. A system of case inflections is the most effective method (allowing word order to be reserved for pragmatic purposes).

How many case choices should there be? Latin has five or six, but in Finnish we find more than a dozen, including terms such as elative 'from the inside of' and illative 'into'. These correspond to prepositions or postpositions (or more complex expressions) in other languages. If a dozen cases have effective use in Finnish, why not elsewhere?

(5) Gender (4.1). Marking the gender of a noun can assist in tracking its path through discourse. Some familiar languages have two or three terms but Swahili employs seven (each gender prefix marked for singular or plural). If this is a suitable gender system for Swahili, why shouldn't it be for other languages (perhaps tacking on a masculine/feminine distinction)?

(6) Definiteness (4.2). Although only a minority of languages have definite and indefinite articles, these can play a major role in clarification. Compare two English sentences:

Looking across men in the village, John is the tall one (all the rest are short)

Looking across men in the village, John is a tall one (Mike, Tom, and Harry are other tall ones)

Since articles *the* and *a* are included, there is no need for the parts in parentheses. But in a language without definiteness-marking articles, a sentence 'John is tall one' would be ambiguous, with the parenthetical bits needed in order to resolve this. Including specification of definiteness in the grammar is always a useful thing.

(7) **Tense, modality, and aspect** (4.3). People do make a few general statements (such as, *Books are easier to read than computer screens*) but most of what is said is reporting the past, or observing the present, or speculating about what is to come. The predicate (generally with a verb as its head) is the core of a clause and it is appropriate that the tense marking should—as in most languages—be attached to the verb. A tense system is a compact way of providing time reference. The alternative is an untidy conglomeration of adverbs such as 'originally', 'just now', 'next', and 'from now on'.

There may be several past tenses, referring to relative temporal distance. Languages vary a good deal in their treatment of what has not yet happened. Having a future term in the tense system is tidy but limited. The more sophisticated alternative is to include a number of modality markers, showing prediction, obligation, necessity, desire, possibility, and so on.

Grammars of Slavic languages typically include a category of aspect. If Vladimir took a long time washing the dishes and while he was doing so Ivan wrote a letter, one would say 'Vladimir washed [imperfective aspect: activity regarded as extended in time] dishes, Ivan wrote [perfective aspect: activity regarded as a unit] letter'. Speakers of Slavic languages value this aspectual contrast, and bemoan its absence from other languages they come to use. Why shouldn't all languages have it?

(8) Evidentiality (4.4). In every language there is need—from time to time—to provide the justification for a statement. A grammatical system of evidentiality makes this obligatory. There may be a two-term system, such as 'reported'/'non-reported' in Estonian, or 'eyewitness'/'non-eyewitness' in Jarawara. Or a much larger one such as that in Tariana: 'visual', 'non-visual', 'inferred', 'assumed', and 'reported'.

Media people have to take care not to attribute to someone a crime before they have been convicted. We often hear things like:

> It was reported that the alleged paedophile had been noticed lurking around the school and it was assumed that he was contemplating further molestations.

If there were an appropriate evidentiality system, the underlined lexemes could all be rendered through the grammar. And, for every statement, its factual basis would have to be specified. Assuming that the language community welcomed such explicitness, this would be of benefit.

(9) Pronoun system (2.5). There is less danger of confusion if non-singular 1st person pronouns include a distinction between 'inclusive' and 'exclusive'.

If John says to Tom 'We (inclusive) have been invited to the party', Tom understands that he has been included in the invitation. But if Tom hears 'We (exclusive) have been invited to the party', the message is that he has been left out. If John should say, in English, *We have been invited to the party*, Tom doesn't know where he stands.

An inclusive/exclusive distinction is something which all languages should share. And how about the number contrasts for pronouns? A {singular, dual, plural} system allows for greater possibilities than plain {singular, plural}. Some languages have a four-term system {singular, dual, paucal (a few), plural (many)}. As an example of the use to which this can be put, I heard an official address a group of Fijian villagers: 'I want to tell *dou* (you paucal) the responsibilities for *nuu* (you plural) . . .' The paucal pronoun, *dou*, was used because he was addressing a group of about a dozen people, and then the plural pronoun, *nuu*, for referring to the responsibilities of everyone in the village (about a hundred of them). Surely a four-term number system in pronouns would find a use in every language?

(10) Causatives (4.7). Many languages have a single causative construction, but others include two. There is always a semantic difference, which varies from language to language. We can list four of these (note that there are more besides):

- **Directness.** In Hindi, there is a contrast between direct and indirect causatives 'I made it happen myself' versus 'I got someone else to make it happen'.
- **Intention.** In Kammu (an Austroasiatic language from Laos), the contrast involves making something happen either intentionally or accidentally; for example, murder versus manslaughter.
- **Volition.** Japanese has a contrast between making a person do something which they are willing or which they are unwilling to do; basically, 'let them do it' versus 'force them to do it'.

- **Involvement.** In Cavineña (a Tacanan language from Bolivia), the two causatives relate to whether or not the causer is also involved in the activity; compare 'I fed (eat-MAKE.UNINVOLVED) him tamales' and 'I invited him to eat (eat-MAKE.INVOLVED) tamales with me'.

Each semantic contrast is useful. Why couldn't it be extended to other languages? Why not go further and suggest that every language might profitably include all these causative specifications?

There are quite a number of other grammatical systems which might well be extended, in their fullest forms, across all languages—three degrees of distance in demonstratives (section 2.5); separate copulas for identity, attribution, possessive, benefaction, and location (3.5), a variety of relative clause and complement clause constructions (3.6), several passives with different meanings (4.6), a range of applicative constructions (4.7). Note that this is far from an exhaustive list.

In summary, why could not every language include explicit marking for declarative mood, several imperatives and interrogatives, several techniques for marking negation, similarly for possession, a system of a dozen or more cases, eight or ten genders, a definiteness distinction, several past tenses and a range of markers for modalities plus perfective/imperfective aspect, four or five evidentiality values, four numbers for pronouns together with inclusive/exclusive, and half-a-dozen causative constructions (plus all the rest)? Why should a language be limited to less than this?

The only limits on a language are the limitations of its users. The human mind is not boundless in its abilities. It can only deal with and process a certain amount of data. No brain could handle more than a fraction of the grammatical detail summarised in the preceding paragraph. Note that this is an empirical observation. It is up to neurolinguists and psycholinguists—if they are worth their salt—to come up with the why and wherefore.

Consider an analogy to a feast. You are invited to the most remarkable buffet with every sort of food and drink that you know, and more besides. Alongside beef, pork, lamb, venison, goat, chicken, turkey, goose, and quail, there is crocodile, camel, tapir, peccary, and opossum. Twenty succulent varieties of fish, cooked in delicate ways. Dozens of vegetables, from mushrooms to palm hearts, squash to brown walnut paste, processed bitter manioc to baby carrots. Twenty of the finest beers, wines of reputation from five continents. spirits galore. Juices from fruits tropical and temperate.

It may be good to look at, but as for eating . . . Your stomach and palate can only extend so far. You pick four small pieces of fish and a sample of four vegetables, plus a tumbler of mango-steen juice. Your neighbour's plate has a different look—several meats, vegetables different from yours, accompanied by a beer from Mexico. So much was on offer, you wish you could sample more, but are held back by physical limitations.

So it is with language and the mind—we are constrained by mental limitations. A grammar is likely to include most, but probably not all, of the recurrent categories, each in a fairly basic form. In one or two instances it may splurge, and indulge in an extended system. But richness of texture in one part of a grammar is likely to go hand-in-hand with a threadbare segment elsewhere. For example, Finnish has a generous array of cases but lacks gender and articles showing definiteness; it has just two numbers for pronouns, no straightforward inclusive/exclusive distinction, and no seman-tic contrast in causatives.

In essence, every grammar includes just a selection of the possible categories, each of variable extent. It is almost as if there were a bag of category balls of different sizes, and each (personified) language puts in its hand and pulls out a limited number. Except that it can't be like that—there must be at least a partial rationale.

Some of the grammatical categories in a language will be inherited, having been present in the ancestor language for that language family. (But then we need to ask why the ancestor language had them.) Some may have been borrowed from a neighbouring language with which there is close social and linguistic contact. (But then, why did that language have them?)

There can be external reasons for a language having or not having certain categories. For instance, a grammatical system 'high'/'low' (as illustrated for Hua at the beginning of chapter 2) or 'up'/'down' (described for Dyirbal in section 5.4) are only likely to be found in languages spoken in hilly country. Section 4.5 explained how communities lacking any habit of competitiveness are unlikely to include a comparative construction in their grammars.

But all peoples recognise a distinction between male and female sex, which can be the basis for a grammatical system of gender. Everyone needs to know the time of an event, which can be neatly codified through a grammatical system of tense. There are many conundrums concerning language which linguistics needs to confront. Why languages have the grammatical categories they do is one of them.

As a language changes over time, a common development is for lexical words to become grammatical items. A set of temporal adverbs may reduce to affixes, and constitute themselves into a grammatical system of tense. Forms such as 'seen', 'heard', and 'told' may reduce to become grammatical markers of evidentiality. A bevy of postpositions (which were separate words) may become affixes, added to an already existing case system.

Once a language has expanded its grammar in one direction, there is less scope for extension and innovation elsewhere, within the overall gamut of how much complexity a grammar may handle, given the limitations of the human brain.

Language is not a chaos of words; it needs an ordered framework within which to operate. The underlying structure is made up of a principled network of semantic elements. Lexical items are linked together by grammatical systems (from which a choice must be made). These provide the fixed points around which the message is articulated.

8.2　What can be said

Is it the case that anything which can be said in one language may be rendered—in an intelligible and reasonably straightforward manner—into another? We can examine grammar first, and then lexicon.

Most terms in grammatical systems can be provided with a short lexical paraphrase. Recent past tense is 'just a short while ago'. Eyewitness evidential is 'I saw it myself'. First person plural inclusive pronoun is 'us (including you)'. The Intention causatives are 'I made it happen deliberately' or 'accidentally'.

But not all of them can be. One particularly difficult category is possession. In Dyirbal, for instance, inalienable possession is shown just by apposition of whole and part nouns, whereas alienable possession (ownership) is marked by genitive suffix -ngu on the possessor. With body part noun *jarra* 'thigh' and verb *gayñjan* 'broke', we get:

INALIENABLE	Jani jarra gayñjan	'John's thigh broke'
ALIENABLE	Jani-ngu jarra gayñjan	'John's thigh broke'

The inalienable construction states that John's own thigh (a part of his body) has broken, whereas for the alienable one it is something external—perhaps the thigh of an animal he has killed and is preparing to cook.

Considerable circumlocution is required in translating these possessive constructions. An even greater challenge concerns trying to explicitly render into another language the perfective/imperfective aspect system, typical of Slavic (section 4.3).

Looking now at the lexicon, sentences involving everyday words are readily translatable; for example 'The baby laughed', 'The dog chased the rat', and 'The woman showed a beautiful flower to her husband'. Some events may be viewed from different angles: whereas in English one states that a person caught a bad cold, other languages say that a bad cold caught the person (which, when you think about it, is a pretty reasonable description).

Going beyond this, every language has words which reflect the particular culture of its speakers, and it is these which may pose problems of translation. Let me illustrate from personal experience. First, a little background is needed.

In traditional times, an Australian Aboriginal tribe was basically egalitarian, with no formalised social hierarchy. For example, there was no 'chief'. Senior men and women who had accumulated skills and knowledge would consult together about some important matter, and arrive at a decision by consensus.

The Europeans who invaded Aboriginal lands during the nineteenth century were interested in raising cattle and finding gold. The indigenous people fought hard but were soon defeated.

(As they told me, spears were no match for guns.) The most belligerent Aborigines were killed, with the remainder permitted to survive under strict conditions. The local policeman would select a docile old Aborigine (often, but not always, of an Uncle Tom disposition) and dub him 'king', bestowing a moon-shaped plate to hang around the neck on which was inscribed 'King of the <whatever> tribe'. The duties of the 'king' were to keep his 'subjects' in order and be responsible to the police for doing so. In fact the Aboriginal people just got on with their own lives, as best they could, and more-or-less ignored the 'king'.

An old Dyirbal man, called in English Jim Robertson, was presented with a moon plate by the police at Ravenshoe around 1920. When he died it went back to the police station. Then in 1997, the police decided to present it to the Dyirbal descendants, in a grand ceremony. Not realising the demeaning and racist overtones of the king plate, the people who identified as being ethnically Dyirbal were very pleased about this and wished to make a speech of acceptance in Dyirbal. The difficulty was that they only knew a few words of the language, not enough to put together a speech.

I had been learning Dyirbal since 1963, working with fluent speakers (by then all deceased). So the Ravenshoe Aborigines wrote out a speech in English and asked me to translate it into Dyirbal for them. Unfortunately, the modern-day descendants had been completely assimilated to white Australian life, so that the sentiments expressed were entirely different from those of their now long-past culture. The following is a segment of what they sent me:

(a) Jim Robertson was our chief.

(b) He was an honest man.

(c) He received this moon plate from the police in 1920.

(d) The moon plate was a symbol of respect for the chief.

Sentence (c) was open to translation, becoming: 'The police (*bulijiman*, an established loan in Dyirbal from English *policeman*) presented him with this plate (*bilirr*, another established loan, from *plate*). But the remaining three sentences involve European-type concepts which cannot be expressed in Dyirbal in a coherent manner. We can discuss them one at a time.

(a) chief. The difficulty here is that there was no such thing as a unique 'chief'. *Gubi* 'wise man, Aboriginal doctor' was used of someone who was a good hunter (*ngirringgal*). and was experienced, knowing how to do things (*jilbay*). A gubi had curative powers and could communicate with spirits. Every tribe had several gubi but not every man achieved this status. It is not known whether Jim Robertson was a gubi.

(b) honest. There is absolutely no corresponding word in Dyirbal. It was simply taken for granted that everyone in the tribe was honest. This was the default state and there was no word to describe it. There were, of course, ways of describing antisocial behaviour—verb *warra-buway* 'tell a lie', and adjective *malnggal* 'answer questions untruthfully, make things up'. It would not be appropriate to translate 'He was honest' by 'He never told a lie, or answered questions untruthfully, or made things up', since it would imply that he had been accused of these misdemeanours, which would provide entirely the wrong impression. Sentence (b) is simply not translatable into Dyirbal in a felicitous manner. (Note that the same would apply for many other small tribal languages in Australia, South America, New Guinea, and no doubt elsewhere.)

(c) **symbol of respect.** Dyirbal has nothing corresponding to English nouns *symbol* and *respect* or verb *respect*. There is adjective *gulugan* 'kind-hearted, respectful towards others'. Saying 'The police were *gulugan* towards Jim Robertson' would be some sort of a translation but a pretty poor one, with only a glancing similarity of meaning.

Thousands of other instances could be provided showing the difficulties of translation between languages which relate to markedly different cultures. But this sample is sufficient to incontrovertibly demonstrate the false nature of the adage 'Everything can be said in every language'.

In summary, languages differ both in what must be said and also in what can be said in them.

8.3 Putting it all together

Lexicon and grammar are mutually dependent, interlocking aspects of a language, but they differ in terms of speakers' awareness.

For most people, a language is its stock of words, the dictionary. If you get the words right, you are speaking the language. Grammar is something speakers have only a vague awareness of, and do not consider to be particularly important.

The grammar of a language is a complex mechanism, a system of systems. Children acquire it naturally, without conscious effort. It appears that the brains of many people who are mentally impaired seamlessly attain a decent grammatical facility. But, as discussed in section 8.1, there are limits to how much grammatical complexity even the cleverest brains can handle. Irregularities (section 5.1) are part of the mix—the more grammatical space they take up, the less room there is for systems which code meaning contrasts.

The lexicon appears to be on a different agenda. It is certainly not the case that the fuller the grammar, the less scope there will be for lexical richness, or vice versa. Vocabulary size relates to memory capacity. Overall, 'educated' people undoubtedly amass a considerable stack of words to play around with (more than are really needed, with a proliferation of semi-synonyms). In a large society, every specialist group employs its own technical terms, be they operators of a cotton loom, or geologists, or paramedics, or farmers. Crooks and thugs have their own 'cant'.

In smaller language communities, the vocabulary will cover every relevant aspect of the social and physical environment. Dyirbal was spoken in rainforest country. Between 1979 and 1992, a botanist and I worked with elderly fluent speakers (both women and men) who had—without exception—a name for every plant. We gathered information on more than 700 trees, vines, grasses, and so on, recording for each the scientific name, the common name in English (if there is one), plus name and gender in Dyirbal, including dialectal variants.

There is a myth—especially prevalent among English-speakers— that the human brain has room only for one language. The dogma is that if you try to teach a second language to a child, it will usurp some of the mental space needed for the mother tongue. Nothing could be more mistaken. When a child (or adult) is explicitly exposed to some of the structural patterns in another language, it sharpens their perception of their own way of speaking. What had previously been unconscious ability—the facility of speaking grammatically—may enter into the realm of awareness.

Many people employ just one language in the course of everyday living. For others there is more, and this can have varying manifestations. A number of speech communities exhibit 'diglossia', where two varieties of a language are used under different circumstances. This is found in Switzerland, where the local dialect of Swiss German is used in informal and High German in formal settings. The two varieties differ only a little in grammar, perhaps a little more in lexicon.

Then there are communities where one must adopt a special speech style in certain situations. Dyirbal, for instance, has a Jalnguy register which is obligatorily employed when in the presence of an actual or classificatory mother-in-law, father-in-law, son-in-law, or daughter-in-law. Jalnguy has exactly the same grammar as the everyday speech style, but every lexeme is different. There aren't as many of them, though, since Jalnguy generally has a single generic term corresponding to a host of specific labels in the everyday style. For example, eighteen names for types of frog are collectively rendered by *juramu* 'frog' in Jalnguy.

Speakers of Swiss German and of Dyirbal effectively each have just a-language-and-a-bit. But how about, say, of a speaker of Vietnamese who immigrates to America and learns English? What often happens is that each language is confined to a limited sphere—Vietnamese in the home and with friends, English in the work place and in formal contexts. Moreover, the immigrant is not able to employ either language in the other sphere. They would not know how to speak in English to family (even though they also use that language outside the home). Two languages are in use, but in complementary circumstances.

Due to a combination of shared genetic origin and cultural context, two distinct languages may show considerable similarity in both grammatical structure and vocabulary. Dutch and German, for instance, share many construction types and a considerable number of lexical cognates. Being bilingual in these two languages is an achievement, but it can scarcely be compared with having fluency in both Welsh and Mandarin Chinese, languages with entirely different phonology, grammar, and lexicon.

Only a small minority of people are truly competent in two (or more) languages which are totally dissimilar. How can this be compatible with what was said before: that the brain can only handle a limited amount of grammatical complexity? In section 8.1 we asked why a language (the 'maximal language') could not include all grammatical categories, each in its most expansive form—a dozen or more cases, eight or ten genders, several past tenses, four or five evidentials, half-a-dozen causatives, several imperatives, interrogatives, and types of possession, and very much more besides. A partial answer is that if you put together the grammatical patterns of Welsh and Mandarin (perhaps throwing in, for good measure, Swahili and Quechua as well) it all adds up to very much less than what would be in the maximal language.

People differ in their mental aptitudes. A few have a special mathematical facility—able to multiply large numbers in their heads, and solving arithmetical problems as a way of dropping off to sleep. And some have exceptional linguistic ability, able to achieve real native-speaker-like competence in several dissimilar languages. Both groups are out of the ordinary. Many of us use a computer even for addition and are basically confined to one language, with perhaps a smattering from one or two similar tongues.

In summary, there are definite limits to the amount of grammatical detail any language can handle. Size of vocabulary is a different, and independent, matter. This does vary with intelligence, application, and retentiveness of memory.

One not infrequently meets people who boast of speaking many languages. When tested they are shown to have a superficial knowledge of most; indeed, I have known people of this ilk who did not have true native-speaker ability in any of their many languages (that is, they made mistakes).

There are just a few exceptional people, with the appropriate kind of mental prowess, who are fully competent in several languages of quite different mien.

Chapter 9

Better for what purpose?

9.1 Better for whom?

Something which is better for one person can be worse for another. A speaker may fail to apply the requisite effort and, as a consequence, pronounces things in a lazy manner. Mary says to John, *I broke a plate this morning*, but she fails to properly articulate the beginning of *broke*, and he hears it as *I woke up late this morning*. (The initial *p* of *plate* is now heard as the final segment of preposition *up* /ʌp/.)

A speaker can be careless, half-pronouncing some sounds, blending others together, letting their voice trail off, and eating the ends of words. Ben intends to tell Sue, *The maid has brought the bedding*, and is puzzled when she replies, *Why should the maid want to buy the bed?* Ben hadn't properly enunciated the initial *br* of *brought*, and he had swallowed the final syllable of *bedding*.

Despite languid pronunciation, the intended message may be understood based on what was said previously, and on what might be expected to be said in this context. As mentioned before, all languages show a measure of redundancy, so that if

Are Some Languages Better than Others? First Edition. R. M. W. Dixon.
© R. M. W. Dixon 2016. Published 2016 by Oxford University Press.

one aspect of the speech event is not ideally executed, other factors may compensate for this.

Nevertheless, what is best from the listener's point of view is for every word to be pronounced clearly and accurately, the possibility of misunderstanding thereby being minimised. In practice, an act of speaking is essentially a compromise, between what is easiest for the speaker and what is most effective for the listener.

A language is always in a state of flux. Endings (for example, suffixes showing case or tense) may cease to be pronounced at the ends of words. Prepositions or postpositions (which were separate words) may be reduced in form and attached to an adjacent word so that they become affixes. Changes of this nature emanate in part from habits of pronunciation.

Change is multifaceted; a given lexeme may develop into a grammatical element in opposite ways in different languages. For example the classifier *mayi* 'vegetable food' occurs in many Australian languages. But in some it has been shortened and become a grammatical affix, the mark of a gender referring to vegetable foodstuffs.

The gender marker is a suffix in Dyirbal (a language which effectively lacks prefixes) by the following development (quoting a typical noun of this gender):

bala	mayi	guway	> bala-m	guway
ARTICLE	classifier	brown.walnut	ARTICLE-GENDER	brown.walnut

Whereas in Dyirbal *mayi* becomes a gender suffix to the article, in other languages it becomes a gender prefix, added to the noun itself (and often also to noun modifiers, and to the verb), as in Yanyuwa:

mayi	budjuwa	>	ma-budjuwa
classifier	lilyroot		GENDER-lilyroot

It is reasonable to enquire whether, when a language changes, it is always for the better. There is no straightforward answer. Every change is undoubtedly beneficial in one way, but it may well engender deleterious changes elsewhere.

The development of inalienably possessed nouns in Jarawara was outlined in section 5.1. Examples include, quoting feminine/masculine:

	ORIGINAL		PRESENT-DAY
'foot'	*tama-ni/tama-ne	>	tame/teme
'face'	*noko-ni/noko-ne	>	noki/noko

The new forms are easier to say—two syllables instead of three. But they are more difficult for the brain to process—gender is shown by alternation of the first vowel in some words and of the second in others, instead of by invariable suffixes -ni/-ne.

Changes can happen naturally, as with inalienably possessed nouns in Jarawara, or they may be purposely engineered. In section 7.2 we examined the consequences of 'gender' being taken out of its role as label for a grammatical category and used more widely to describe female versus male sex. Many application forms now enquire about one's 'gender' whereas before it used to be 'sex'. Some people, apparently, are happier this way; however, there is a price to pay. The implication is that one should now say: 'Noun *Mädchen* 'girl' in German is of neuter gender but refers to a person of female s̶e̶x̶ gender'. This is daft. The moral is that taking a technical term out of its niche may have undesirable repercussions.

Some languages are easier (and thus better) than others for linguists writing grammars and compiling dictionaries, and for applied linguists producing primers and other teaching materials.

A good language, from this point of view, has each word neatly segmentable—by hyphens—into meaning-bearing units. English fits this pattern well. Consider *interest*, which functions as a noun and as a verb. It has quite a few forms, including:

INFLECTIONS	interest-s, interest-ed, interest-ing
DERIVATIONS	
WITH SUFFIXES	interest-free, interest-less, interest-worthy
WITH PREFIX	dis-interest

There are also a couple of prefixes which also require suffix *-ed*, giving *un-interest-ed* and *half-interest-ed*. The root form, *interest*, is clearly visible in each instance, and the word is automatically placed within alphabetical order in a dictionary.

The Australian language Murinypata is of a quite different nature. Each verb has scores of forms, showing person and number of the subject, plus tense, etc. Consider four sample forms for each of two auxiliary verbs, 'arrive' and 'polish':

	'arrive'	'polish'
1sg future	ngurdayecicnu	ngilabilbilinu
2sg future	turduyecicnu	cilabilbilnu
1sg perfect	ngurdañcecic	ngilamilbil
2sg perfect	turdañcecic	cilamilbil

The first part of each verb indicates whether the subject is 1st or 2nd person singular, the middle part is the root, and the last part marks future or perfect. But where do we put the hyphens? What is the form of the root, for each verb? If we can't recognise a root, how can we construct a dictionary? And how on earth can school lessons explaining verbs in Murinypata be constructed?

When teaching a language, one starts from simple structures and gradually builds up from these. In English, *interest* as a noun takes plural ending *-s*. As a verb it takes standard verbal endings *-s*, *-ed*, and *-ing*. Later on, derivational processes are explained, One can have an *interest-free loan* (no interest is charged) and someone may have an *interest-less look* on their face (they couldn't care less). And so on.

In Murinypata, nouns and adjectives are straightforward, and effective school lessons have been produced explaining them. But verbs? It seems that a learner simply has to memorise the paradigm (with scores of forms, only a small sample having been illustrated above) for each of umpteen verbs. It can be seen that Murinypata is not such a good language for linguistic-descriptive and pedagogic purposes.

9.2   For identification

A major role of language, mentioned in section 1.1, is 'assisting in the process of belonging'. Having a name identifies a person to themself, and to others. Bestowing a name is a serious matter, and should not be entered into prematurely. When living among the Jarawara, I one day enquired the name of a few-months-old baby, only to receive the reply *Ini wata-ke-re* 'Her name does not exist'. Infant mortality is high and a child is not accorded a name until it has survived six months or so (and then has an excellent chance of progressing into adulthood).

Naming practices differ across cultures, and can be difficult to transfer. A single name is sufficient in Indonesia, but when

Suhandano came to study at an Australian university, he was told that two names were needed on every one of the many forms to be completed. Thus he became Suhandano Suhandano.

The convention in western countries is to have 'first name' (or given name, or christian name) plus 'last name' (or family name or surname). One or more middle names are entirely optional. The last name is father's last name. When a woman gets married, the normal expectation has been for her to take on the husband's last name, although today educated women are more and more preferring to retain their father's last name.

For the first name, parents can indulge in any whim. Many people do, however, choose to emphasise a sense of belonging by re-using the name of a family member. For example, I was called Robert after my mother's father. My father was given the same first name, William, as his father, and he had the same one as his father (my great-grandfather). In contrast, Lottie and Ian Catford named their daughter Lorna, just because they liked the name. (This is a name which belonged to no family, having been created by R. D. Blackmore for the heroine of his novel *Lorna Doone*, in 1869.) Anyone can make up a name; my own eldest daughter is called Eelsha.

Other cultures have different conventions. In Russia a middle name is required—the patronymic. This is the father's first name plus *-ovich* 'son of' for a boy and *-ovna* 'daughter of' for a girl. Thus the son of *Vladimir Veniaminovich Rudov* is *Mikhail Vladimirovich Rudov* and his daughter is *Anastasia Vladimirovna Rudova* (here the last name bears feminine suffix *-a*).

Whereas Russian names include information about the father's first name, in Spanish the mother's last name (which is her father's last name) is added after the father's last name. The full name of the daughter of *Miguel Alvarez* and *Carmen*

González will be *Maria Alvarez González*. This is how her name will appear on a passport and other official documents, but on a day-to-day basis she is just *Maria Alvarez* (and is placed under 'A' in alphabetical order). If Maria should emigrate from Peru into Brazil she would become *Maria González Alvarez* on formal documents but remain *Maria Alvarez* informally; in Portuguese the mother's last name is placed before the father's last name.

Much name-giving is highly male-oriented. I have a friend who married and took her husband's last name. Then she got divorced, became a feminist, and wanted to have a name which bore no reference to any man. She could have replaced her husband's last name with her maiden name, but that was her father's last name—another man. Her mother's first name had been *Marie* and she adopted as a new last name *Rieschild* (short for *Marie's child*), which is man-free.

A name which is arbitrary simply serves to define the person it is attached to. Motivated names may indicate how and where the person belongs. One of my Dyirbal teachers, George Watson, was *Nyiyija*, a name based on common noun *nyiyi* 'the fine bone in the jaw of an eel', since the eel is a totem of his tribal section.

In Manambu, spoken in the Sepik region of New Guinea, each patrilineal clan has an inventory of proper names, a number of which will be bestowed on a new-born child. In this culture, names are 'owned' and jealously regarded. The story is told of a missionary who began by recounting the story of Adam. 'Hey, that's one of our clan's names, you've stolen it', the people cried, running the missionary out of the village.

It is common practice for a child to be given the name of an ancestor. Sometimes it must be someone who is already dead. In other cultures two people may share the same name. Amongst the Warlpiri, in Central Australia, a child 'acquires a personal name when about two years old, that is, after it has survived the many sicknesses that contribute to the high rate of infant mortality. A boy receives the name of a grandfather, usually of his mother's father, and a girl that of a grandmother, usually of her mother's mother. The grandparent decides, without prompting, to offer the name.' When the grandparent dies, their name is tabooed for a year or so, and the grandchild is then referred to as *gumindjari* 'no name'. After the period of taboo is completed, the grandparent's name is resumed.

A new stage of life is often marked by a new name, as when a western woman adopts her husband's last name to indicate that she has a fresh familial niche. In many African and Australian societies, a special name is bestowed upon a youth when he undergoes the initiation ceremony. Anthropologist A. P. Elkin reports that, in Australia, the initiation name 'is usually taken from a sacred myth; in some tribes, it may be the name of a great dream-time hero. It is so sacred that it is never mentioned except in a whisper on the sacred ground. It is, indeed, a pass word into the eternal, unseen world of ancestral and totemic heroes.' Buddhist initiation rituals involve the adoption of another name. And when a woman becomes a nun, it is natural for her to take on a new name, of holy import.

In essence, a person's name is an inherent part of them. (It is often treated in grammar as inalienably possessed, like a body part.) There are few worse indignities than having one's name misspelled or mispronounced. A name can be informative, indicating its holder's position in their family and in the community. Really, the more informative the better.

9.3 For learning

The consensus is that every child—whatever their ethnic origin—is equally capable of learning any language if brought up in the appropriate cultural setting. Have an Eskimo baby adopted by a family in Barcelona and it will grow up speaking Catalan as fluently as the local children. A Hindi child will have no difficulty mastering the tones of Mandarin, nor a Swahili child the cases of Finnish.

A language is not a self-contained entity which can be learnt in the same way as, say, symbolic logic. Language is one element—perhaps the most important one—in the fabric of a human society. A language is learnt together with, and interrelated with, every other aspect of the culture to which it pertains. How to think, how to behave, what can acceptably be done in which circumstances. This knowledge—cultural and linguistic intertwined—is acquired naturally and gradually by the child.

Intricate linguistic details can only be mastered once a suitable cultural understanding is achieved. In order to count in Thai, an appropriate 'numeral classifier' must be included, as in:

măa   săam   tua
dog   three   classifier(animals)
'three dogs'

Some classifiers have a general meaning; for example, *tua* is used of animals, of furniture with legs, and of clothing. Others are rather specialised; for instance, *chyag* is a classifier for elephants in their ceremonial, religious function. (In contrast, an elephant in a zoo would just take *tua*.) Children master the mechanics of the grammar at an early age—that a number word must be followed by a classifier. However, getting to know details of which classifier is used with which noun is a gradual process. The honorific classifier for elephants, *chyag*, will not enter a speaker's competence until they become fully aware—perhaps only in early adulthood—of the role of elephants in Thai ceremonies and religion.

All languages are equally suitable for being learnt (to be spoken) by a child. Any child will acquire reasonable competence in a language to which it is exposed, although some will reach a certain level at a slightly earlier age than others. Relevant factors are (among others) the child's intelligence, their innate language aptitude, the familial setting in which they are placed, and the complexity of the language.

The spoken mode is everywhere the major manifestation of language. But in many societies reading and writing are also important, and languages do differ a great deal in how easy it is to master the written mode. If the writing system is alphabetic, the ideal situation is for each phoneme (section 2.2) to be represented by a single letter in the orthography. With a couple of minor exceptions, this is the case for Spanish. Once you know how to pronounce a word, you know how to write it; and once you know how to write a word, you know how to pronounce it.

The English writing system is quite different, and much harder to master. A single sound may be written in many different ways. For example, each of the following nine words ends in the same diphthong (phonetically /ou/), although written differently: *owe, sew, toe, blow, though, cocoa, disco, depot, tableaux*. In the opposite direction, the same letters may indicate different sounds; for instance, each of the following words ends in *-ood*, but this represents three different vowels: *good* /gud/, *food* /fuːd/, *blood* /blʌd/.

Many native speakers never master the English writing system absolutely perfectly. After a lifetime of correction I still sometimes write *occassion* when it should be *occasion*. Why doesn't it have a double *s*, parallel to *succession*? Why can't I write *inovate* with a single *n*, by analogy with *inundate*, which has just one *n*? *Questionaire* is another spelling I get wrong—there should be two *n*'s. But *concessionnaire* and *concessionaire* are acceptable alternative spellings; why not *questionnaire* and *questionaire*?

Most often, the child first encounters a word in the spoken mode, and learns how to pronounce it. As a second step, they have to learn how to spell it. There are, of course, some groupings which help—*hood*, *stood*, and *wood* have the same vowel as *good*, while *mood*, *rood*, and *brood* have the same one as *food*, and *flood* has the same one as *blood*.

A few less common words may be encountered first in written form. There could then be difficulty in learning how to pronounce them, especially if the pronunciation is rather different from what might be expected from the written form. As an example, it took me until about the age of 40 to learn how to pronounce *heir* 'someone who will inherit'. I felt that it should be spoken with an *h*, and varied between /heə/, the same as *hair* and *hare*, /hiə/, the same as *here*, and /haiə/, the same as *hire*. I eventually realised that there is no *h* in the pronunciation; *heir* is just a diphthong, /eə/, identical to *air*. (In an *r*-full dialect, each of these words would end in *r*.)

In summary, English is no more difficult or easy than any other language to learn to speak. But the eccentric orthography poses a challenge even for first-language (L1) learners. For a foreigner attempting to acquire English as a second language (L2), the difficulties can be frightening. The situation is exacerbated when the L2 speaker learns words first in written form and only later tries to convert this into speaking (this is much harder than the other way round).

Are some languages easier to learn, as an L2, than others? This is not an easy question to answer. To properly master a language, one must assimilate the culture of which it is a part. One should live in a community where the language is L1, hear it spoken all around, try to speak it oneself as much as possible, and ask for one's errors to be corrected. One should take part in community life, noting the ways in which the language is used, and its pragmatic effects. For a child L2-learner this should be sufficient. But for an adult—past the age at which language learning is entirely natural—it has been shown that proficiency is greatly increased when language immersion is augmented by explicit lessons in grammar.

It is, of course, easiest to learn another language-plus-culture which is most similar to one's own. For a Punjabi speaker, Marathi will be far more straightforward than Vietnamese or Welsh or Quechua. There are many lexical cognates and similar grammatical categories and construction types. The cultural backgrounds are very similar, and the ways in which language is used within them—techniques for enquiring, persuading, cajoling, expostulating.

If the L2 is culturally distant from the L1, then grammatical similarities may play a role (although perhaps not a major one) in assisting the learning process. Mastering an L2 with a case system may be a trifle less demanding for someone whose L1 has cases, than for someone else whose L1 lacks them. Similarly for genders, articles, tenses, comparative constructions, and so on.

However, superficial similarity may be deceptive. L2 and L1 might both have articles, but employed in significantly different ways; for example, one language may use articles with names of places while the other doesn't. It may be easier for someone from an article-less L1 to master the articles in an L2, than for someone who has a partly similar and partly different system of articles.

Are there any features which are particularly resistant to being learned, and others which are rather open to being learned? A system of tones seems to be an example of the former. Not that there is anything inherently difficult in tones; children acquire them naturally and effortlessly. But to many (although by no means all) adult L2-learners, tones appear to be something alien and thus rather frightening. A kind of psychological barrier is erected.

Some languages have disjunctive clause linking; for example, in English: *At the wedding, Mary will sing or John will dance.* Others lack this and employ 'maybe'; thus 'Maybe Mary will sing, maybe John will dance'. It seems that a disjunctive construction is highly learnable. Speakers of an 'or'-less L1 have no difficulty in mastering disjunction in an L2. Indeed, as noted in section 3.6, small language communities in South America and Australia (and no doubt in other regions as well) so appreciate disjunction in a colonial L2 that they typically borrow the construction into their L1s.

Leaving aside similarities of linguistic structure and inter-woven culture, are there some well-developed languages which are easier than others to be learnt? These would be languages of an 'ideal' character, as outlined in the next chapter. Such languages include all the main grammatical categories, in modest extent. However, surmounting this basic infrastructure, each language is likely to exert its personality, as it were, by adding a number of individual intricacies. And these will vary in how learnable they are.

Towards the end of section 6.3, there was mention of McWhorter's suggestion that recently-developed creoles—while still bona fide languages—have only had time to develop a moderate degree of complexity. They are relatively simple. There is less to learn, and thus they are quite easy to learn.

Consider, for instance, Tok Pisin, which is a lingua franca over most of Papua New Guinea. This is in no way 'primitive'; it has three numbers in pronouns, generally an inclusive/exclusive distinction, a possessive construction marked by *bilong* (similar to English *of*), relative clause and complement clause constructions, much compounding, and a great deal more. But still it is easier to master than the 700 or so indigenous languages, which show demanding complexities (reflecting the culture of which they are a part). Interestingly, children often speak first in Tok Pisin, adding the local language by the age of 5 or 6.

9.4   What people miss

Almost everyone has a particular attachment to their native tongue (the L1). When they go to live within a different language community, there are generally a few features of the L1—lacking in the L2 which they now use on a daily basis—which they miss. It can be interesting to investigate this.

I asked a number of colleagues from non-English-speaking backgrounds (and now working in the Language and Culture Research Centre at James Cook University in Australia) what they particularly missed. Here is a selection of the responses.

(a) Informal and formal 2nd person singular pronouns. In French, one uses *tu* 'you' to servants, children, relatives, and close friends, but *vous* 'you' otherwise. When adults first meet, they will address each other as *vous*. Once a degree of camaraderie develops, this may be replaced by *tu*.

A number of languages have informal/formal varieties of 'you', similar to tu/vous in French. These include *esi/esis* in Greek, *du/Sie* in German, *ty/vy* in Russian, *sina/teie* in Estonian, and *du/ni* in Swedish. This contrast is very hard to render in languages which lack it.

For example, the English translation of Ingmar Bergman's film script *Wild Strawberries* includes the following exchange between a professor and his long-time housekeeper:

PROFESSOR: Don't you think that we who have known each other for two generations could drop formality and say '*du*' to each other?

AGDA: No, I really don't think so...I beg to be excused from all intimacies. It's all right the way it is now between us.

PROFESSOR: But, dear Miss Agda, we are old now.

AGDA: Speak for yourself Professor. A woman has to think of her reputation, and what would other people say if the two of us suddenly started to say '*du*' to each other?

This would be unintelligible without some knowledge of the cultural context.

An L1 speaker of Greek, and another of French, explained that they missed the informal/formal contrast within 'you' because there was nothing to encode social distance, something they were familiar with and felt the need of. That is, there was a cultural parameter, which the single pronoun *you* in English does not illuminate.

However, in particular circumstances the lack of an obligatory formal/informal distinction may be considered an advantage. When a Swedish journalist met a German writer, she asked that the interview should be conducted in English (although she speaks German fluently) simply to avoid a decision concerning whether to use *du* or *Sie*.

(b) Idioms. Every language has a stock of idiomatic expressions, but their function varies from culture to culture. 'What I miss about Russian', one L1 speaker confided, 'is its colourful idioms. These often function as ice-breakers, and release interpersonal tension; they are frequently accompanied by laughter.'

This is something that an L2 learner is unlikely to fully master. Each language has its personalised features, which assist interaction and cooperation.

(c) Emotive lexemes. An L1 speaker of Greek said that she missed words expressing 'deep emotions of joy, pleasure, love, pain' which cannot easily be rendered in English. Here are a couple of examples:

There was a big celebration at home in Greece for my sister's birthday. I was feeling terribly homesick. When I met with my friend in Cairns, I told her 'I am sad because I am missing home'. But the word 'sad' did not describe fully the emotion that I was experiencing. What I really felt at the moment was 'kaimós' (καημός), i.e. a great sadness, deep inside me, for being away from home, and a strong desire—that couldn't be fulfilled—to be back there with my beloved ones.

I was speaking with my girlfriends about my ex-partner with whom I was deeply in love. I referred to my emotions for him as 'love' or 'crush' but these words were not enough; what I felt for him was even more passionate and intense. It was 'kapsúra' (καψούρα).

A speaker of Brazilian Portuguese misses *saudades*:

Saudades is what you feel when thinking of someone who is far away or dead and whom you might not see again. It can be a tragic feeling of loss, or just mild nostalgia, 'missing' someone or something. It is also a very nice way of finishing a letter—when I write *saudades* to a dear friend, it means that they mean a lot to me, and I am missing them, and would like to get back the good times we had together. The feeling of *saudades* is bitter-sweet.

In section 1.1, 'used to display emotion' was highlighted as a major function of language. Greek and Portuguese are particularly rich in this regard.

(d) Ease of expression. A colleague from Ethiopia grew up with Amharic and Wolaitta, languages in which the verb bears bound pronominal affixes indicating core arguments, while nouns and pronouns (which can occur in any order before the verb) take case endings showing their functions within the clause. She comments:

I miss the ease with which I can formulate my thoughts, in Amharic and Wolaitta. The verb, and especially how the forms of pronouns, nouns and proper names indicate the actor and the affected participant/entity. So I do not need to be concerned about the sequence in which the words occur or about leaving one or more of the nominal constituents to be understood.

This shows that the rather complex word structures of Amharic and Wolaitta provide for welcome freedom in the way a sentence is put together.

9.5   What might be the consequences?

Imagine a large island, within which are six nations, each with its own culture and language. There is inter-nation trade, a little cross-marriage, plenty of artistic and sporting festivals, plus a few skirmishes over the location of borders (but nothing like an all-out war). Things are in a state of equilibrium for thousands of years.

Then, all of a sudden, two ambitious and ruthless leaders arise, one in the northernmost nation, N, and one in the southernmost one, S. Each is power-hungry, determined to impose his nation's rule over the whole island. The intention is that his nation's laws should apply everywhere, that their culture should dominate, and also their language.

Who will win out? The leaders of both N and S are equally shrewd and scheming. Their armies and armaments are of roughly equal capability, their generals of roughly equal skill and ferocity. To an outside observer, a major difference is in their languages.

In its grammar, the language of N is pretty similar to those of the four intermediate nations, with three genders, three tenses, two possessive constructions, a single technique for forming negation. That of S is markedly different, with eight genders, no tenses, six types of possession, and a tangle of ways for negating. But perhaps the most significant difference is in the phonologies of the languages. For N there are five vowels and twenty consonants, plus straightforward word structures CV, CVCV, CVCVCV, etc. For example, 'water' is *ga*, 'fire' is *yugo*, 'turtle' is *bajige*. The other four languages have similar phonologies.

In contrast, S has fifteen vowels and forty consonants, plus a word structure which can begin and end with sequences of consonants. Thus, *vsrœðl* is 'water', *prumbr* is 'fire' and for 'turtle' the word is *bjмlngip*. Many people from the other five nations can communicate in two or three of their languages. Speakers of the S language learn some of the others—they have to, since virtually no one from outside the S nation learns that language. It is simply too hard.

When historians search for why the N nation won the great war that engulfed that large island, some speak about the pincer-movement of attack, others invoke ambushes in deep ravines. A few of the shrewder scholars bring in the matter of language. How the four nations in the middle preferred to surrender to N— rather than to S—and to join up with them, because they found the language of N to be euphonic and congenial, as opposed to that of S, which was considered harsh and alien.

In actual situations, language is unlikely to be the overriding factor. Tactics, weaponry, ruthlessness will be paramount. But language may still play a role, albeit a minor one. A language which is 'better' (in a way to be characterised in the next chapter) may be a significant aid in conquering. (And perhaps also for missionising, which involves conquering minds.)

A number of other functions of language were outlined in section 1.1. To facilitate cooperative effort, clear marking of speech acts is an advantage, especially commands and other techniques for getting things done. Aesthetic expression is aided by rhythmic word structures, alliterative patterns, and possibilities for word play. Scientific thought and argumentation require grammatical techniques for all kinds of conjunction, disjunction, purpose, consequence, and result. Smooth discourse results from judicious employment of pronouns, demonstratives, and anaphoric techniques. Bombastic rhetoric is needed for inveighing people into embracing a political or religious doctrine.

The next chapter provides a summation and integration of what has been discussed thus far.

Chapter 10
An ideal language

Diversity is the heartspring of every aspect of the world we live in. This applies especially for language. There is today an immense variety of languages, each with its own distinctive and endearing character. A language is the repository of history and legends, laws and conventions—of the accumulated knowledge of the society it serves. Each fulfils its purpose in its own way.

We here summarise some of the features—almost all discussed in previous chapters—which should ideally be present in every language, to ensure that it is an effective vehicle for identification, cooperation, communication, argumentation, and so on.

The sections which follow indicate the set of features which might be called the infrastructure of a language. These are generally grammatical categories of modest extent, such as three genders, three tenses, and six cases. Each individual language will add to these basics what one might call 'luxuries', according to its own bent. Perhaps eight genders in one instance, seven tenses in another, twelve cases in yet another. The number of luxuries in any one language will necessarily be limited by the capabilities of the human brain (see chapter 8).

Are Some Languages Better than Others? First Edition. R. M. W. Dixon.
© R. M. W. Dixon 2016. Published 2016 by Oxford University Press.

Consider the following analogy. Every western-style house should have four basic rooms but to these can be added luxuries of different kinds:

BASICS	LUXURIES
bathroom with bath or shower	spa bath
kitchen with stove and refrigerator	freezer, dish-washer
bedroom with bed and chair	en suite, walk-in wardrobe
living room with table and chairs	separate dining room
	additional rooms: more bedrooms, nursery, study, conservatory, patio, etc.

Families with about the same capital will build houses all of which include the basics but which are of quite different character. This is by virtue of the diverse luxuries chosen. One will opt for a walk-in wardrobe and en suite, one for a nursery, another for a patio. (No one can afford more than a selection of the possible luxuries.)

So it is with languages. After establishing the basics, a limited balance of luxuries will be added, different for each language, creating the fine array of linguistic designs which grace the world today. There should not be too much complexity, or learning the language may be difficult for an outsider. And overall there should not be an excess of efficiency; a goodly amount of redundancy is desirable if the language is to be comprehensible despite 'channel noise' and other distractions.

The luxuries, and to some extent the way the basics are realised, will relate to the profile of the language—whether it has simple or complex word structure, whether grammatical elements are segmentable affixes or fused together. And also to the nature of the society which the language serves, and the terrain in which it is spoken. Deferential pronouns are needed where there is a fine-tuned social hierarchy. And demonstratives indicating height as well as distance are helpful for a language spoken in the mountains.

Section 10.1 deals with general features, some to avoid and a couple to embrace, before sections 10.2–3 list phonological and grammatical features, and section 10.4 lexical ones, for an ideal language. There are some concluding comments in section 10.5.

A most important point to be stressed before you read further is that the forty-two features presented in the remainder of this chapter simply reflect my opinion. They are most certainly not set in stone. You should think about and assess each one, modifying (or even deleting) it as you judge appropriate. And you may well choose to add further features.

10.1   General features

First of all, six features to be avoided.

1. Do not have intonation as the only mark of a grammatical distinction. For example, Mary says, *The plumber's coming at 8 o'clock in the morning?* John responds, *Is he?* Mary then says, irritably, *I don't know, I was asking you. That was a question.* There may have been some background noise—perhaps a tap running—and John hadn't picked up the rising intonation of Mary's (confirmation-expecting) question.

Quite apart from the possibility of engendering confusion, using intonation for grammatical marking means that it is not so available for pragmatic and emotive purposes (for instance, showing dismay, or scorn, or affection).

2. **Do not use the ordering of words as the only mark of a grammatical property.** A language which has explicit marking for what is subject and what is object—for example, by a system of cases—is able to use word order to indicate what is the topic running through a section of discourse, or what is the focus of attention in a particular clause, or for other pragmatic purposes. All this is lost for a language like English where subject and object functions can only be shown by the relative placement of words; for example *Mary*SUBJECT *saw John*OBJECT.

In section 9.4, a scholar whose native languages include cases, and bound pronouns attached to the verb, said that, when speaking English, 'I miss the ease with which I can formulate my thoughts.' That is, she deplores the fact that in English words have to be placed in a fixed order to show grammatical relations, thus missing the ability to deploy ordering for pragmatic purposes.

Some languages simply juxtapose words to show possession; either 'John car' or 'car John' (depending on the language) indicates 'John's car' (section 3.3 and feature 21 below). And whereas most languages employ a copula for relations of identity and attribution, in others juxtaposition is all we find, saying 'My father a lawyer' and 'My daughter clever' (section 3.5 and feature 24). In each instance, explicit marking is to be preferred.

3. **Have few or no homonyms.** If two lexemes with quite different meanings have the same form there is clearly danger of confusion (section 7.2). This applies the least when the two words are used in quite different textual and situational contexts, as with English *bank* (sloping ground versus financial institution). It can be a major impediment to communication when the two words occur

in the same context, as with *funny* (amusing or peculiar), *hot* (of temperature or of spiciness), and *curious* (inquisitive or unusual).

As a lad of 7 or 8 (in the mid-1940s) I heard on the radio about a 'ground nuts scheme' in East Africa. What did it mean? I was aware that grinding was a process often applied to nuts. All the nuts I'd seen growing had been on trees, but I supposed that there might be some nuts which grew on the ground. Either homonym seemed plausible in the context. It was just a case of the English language not being, in this instance, a very good vehicle for communication.

Grammatical homonymy is also undesirable. English goes to town on this, with suffix *-s* marking (a) 'present tense' on a verb with 3rd person singular subject; (b) plural on a noun; and (c) possessor on a noun (then generally written with an apostrophe). Examples of possible ambiguities were provided, in section 7.2). The *-s* on *changes* could be sense (a) or (b) in the two interpretations of *The Dutch study changes on a daily basis*. The *-s* on *deacons* could be sense (b) or (c) in *The vicar's wife baked a cake and the deacons baked scones*. And the *-s* on *shows* could be sense (a) or (c) in *The circus show(')s acrobats care*. (These ambiguities also depend on so many lexemes in English undertaking 'double duty', as members of two or more word classes—see feature 36 in section 10.4.)

4. **Avoid pairs of lexemes with very similar pronunciations but different meanings, which belong to the same semantic field.** A canonical example of this is English pairs extending from *thirteen* /θəːtiːn/, and *thirty* /θəːti/ on up to *nineteen* /naintiːn/ and *ninety* /nainti/. These are a perpetual source of confusion. Not being sure whether one has properly heard the end of the

word, explication is typically required: *Did you mean one-three or three-zero?*

5. Have a minimum of irregularities. The human brain can only handle a limited amount of grammatical information, and it is important that every portion of it should convey meanings. Irregularities do not do this (section 5.1). Irregularities typically detail a host of alternative ways for expressing a grammatical feature which could be better dealt with in a single homogeneous manner.

Irregularities frequently reflect the history of a language, and there is a steady and gradual tendency to regularise them. English strong verbs provide a good example: some people still use the old forms *dreamt* and *lit* while others prefer regularised *dreamed* and *lighted*. The language will be easier to learn and to use once all verbs inflect in the same way—when *given* and *gave* have been replaced by *gived*, *sung* and *sang* by *singed*, and *left* by *leaved*.

However, irregularities are useful when they help avoid what might otherwise be an ambiguity. The regular plural ending in English is *-s*, but (as just described under feature 3) this is homonymous with the possessive suffix *-s*, and can be confused with it. However, English retains just a few archaic plural forms—including *men*, *women*, and *children*—and these can serve to avoid possible ambiguities. Consider the two sentences:

1 The children love$_{\text{VERB}}$ surprises$_{\text{NOUN}}$
2 The child's love$_{\text{NOUN}}$ surprises$_{\text{VERB}}$

If the irregular *children* were replaced by the regular plural *childs*, then sentence 1 would become *The childs love surprises*, which is identical to sentence 2 (except for the apostrophe, which does not occur in speaking).

6. Avoid having an orthography which does not have a simple correspondence between contrastive sounds (phonemes) and letters of the alphabet. In section 1.4, 'The truth about writing', it was pointed out that many small societies had no original need for writing. A fair number of them have now had orthographies devised for their languages, and these are uniformly of an ideal nature, with a one-to-one correspondence between phonemes and letters. Once you know how to pronounce a word, you know how to write it, and vice versa.

Many large-scale languages have decent orthographies; Spanish was mentioned in section 9.3. But others lack such a thing, English being a prime culprit. Someone who wants to learn British English is told that *bomb* is pronounced /bɔm/ (the final *b* being lost). The learner then encounters *comb* and assumes that, since it is similar in spelling to *bomb*, it has the same vowel, giving /kɔm/. No, that is incorrect. *Comb* has a diphthong, /koum/, the same as in *home*, /houm/. Soon after, *come* appears. Spelt—or spelled—like *home* and presumably involving the same diphthong. No, once again. *Come* has a different vowel, /kʌm/, the same as that in *dumb*, /dʌm/.

Why not change the orthography of English to make it more rational? A major difficulty is that the major dialects have slightly different vowel systems. For example, *lot* and *cloth* have the same vowel in Standard British pronunciation, but are different in General American. Contrarywise, *cloth* and *thought* have the same vowel in American but differ in British. If vowel spelling were rationalised it would give slightly different results for the major dialects. That is, they would be written differently. It is perhaps preferable to have a single irrational vowel system (which does reflect the history of the language), rather than several slightly different fully rational ones.

Nevertheless, changes can and should be made. To begin with, letters *q*, *x*, and *c* could be done away with, the sounds /k/ and /s/ always being written as *k* and *s*. *Circus* and *quixotic* would become *sirkus* amd *kwiksotic* respectively. Letter *g* should be reserved for the sound /g/ (so-called 'hard *g*'), as in *gear* and not used for /dʒ/ ('soft *g*'), which should always be written *j*, as it is now in *jealous*; that is, *general* and *ginger* would become *jeneral* and *jinjer*.

Also, it should not be beyond the capabilities of a group of insightful scholars to devise a new and more rational system of vowel letters which could be interpreted in slightly different ways for the various major dialects. Such changes would make English easier to learn and to use.

We can now mention a couple of general features which should be welcomed.

7. **Have one or more productive processes of reduplication.** The process of reduplication occurs in most languages of the world (but is, surprisingly, rather rare in the familiar languages of Europe). It involves repeating all or part of a word form either before or after it (or, sometimes, in the middle) and carries any of a wide range of meanings.

In Indonesian, full reduplication of a noun carries plural meaning:

rumah 'house'	rumah-rumah 'houses'
perubahan 'change'	perubahan-perubahan 'changes'

Dyirbal has full reduplication of a noun, also indicating plurality:

gundulu 'cassowary'	gundulu-gundulu 'cassowaries'

Verbs in Dyirbal just reduplicate the first two syllables and the meaning is 'do to excess':

miyandañu 'laugh'   miya-miyandañu 'laugh too heartily'

A verb in Jarawara may take any of three kinds of reduplication; these can be illustrated with *joko* 'push':

- initial syllable, 'do a little bit'   jo-joko 'push a bit'
- first two syllables, 'do with force'   joko-joko 'give a tremendous shove to'
- last syllable, 'many participants'   joko-ko 'push lots of things'

Either of the first two processes may be combined with the third—*jo-jojo-ko* 'push lots of things a bit', *joko-joko-ko* 'give lots of things a tremendous shove'.

In Mandarin Chinese, verbs and adjectives are rather similar in their grammatical properties. One criterion for distinguishing them is the meanings of reduplication. With a verb this indicates 'do a little bit':

dòng 'to move'   dòng-dòng 'to move a little'

In contrast, when an adjective is reduplicated, the semantic effect is intensification of the quality, as in:

hóng 'red'   hóng-hóng 'vividly red'

Reduplication carries many diverse meanings across the world's languages. With nouns it may indicate 'collective' or 'dispersed' or 'diminutive' and with verbs 'do repeatedly', 'do intensively', or 'happen continuously', among other senses.

Reduplication is a straightforward and easy way of showing meaning, not involving the addition of an affix. It is a highly desirable feature, for any language.

8. Have ways of forming augmentatives and diminutives. Many languages have a set of affixes which, when added to a noun or adjective, indicate 'a large version of' and a 'small version of'. From *sapo* 'toad' in Portuguese can be derived augmentative *sapão* 'a great big toad' and diminutive *sapinho* 'a tiny little toad'.

Diminutive may not always refer to size at all but can simply add a warm and endearing nuance. This applies to suffix *-ito/-ita* in Spanish:

> In a bakery one might say *Deme una barrita de pan* 'give me a loaf of bread', which is merely a friendly equivalent of *Deme una barra de pan*. This use of the diminutive does not imply small-ness but merely signals the speaker's attitude to the hearer.

Some of the people who were asked what they missed from their L1 when speaking English (section 9.4) singled out in particular diminutives and augmentatives. When the former are added to proper names they can convey a loving intimacy. These word-forming processes are most useful for fulfilling the 'displaying emotions' function of a language (section 1.1).

10.2 Phonology

There should be sufficient phonological contrasts to convey necessary meaning distinctions, but not so many as to make the language more difficult than the norm to easily enunciate, or for a listener to readily comprehend.

9. Vowels. The most appropriate number of vowels is that which is most common across the world's languages, five. Prototypically they are /i/, /e/, /a/, /o/, and /u/. This is the vowel system of Latin, echoed in the alphabet for English, but quite different from the actual system of seven short and five long vowels in British English today (section 2.2).

It seems that five is the ideal number of vowels such that the articulatory and acoustic distances between them can be readily processed by speaker and hearer. A three- or four-vowel system is, of course, also manageable, but having fewer choices available for the vowel slots of a word means that words have to be longer, or there will be more homonyms, or both.

Having more than five vowels can be regarded as a luxury for the native speaker, but may be an impediment for an adult learner. One native speaker of Dutch (and a linguist to boot) has spent five years in Australia without managing the contrast between vowels /ʌ/ and /ɔ/. She pronounces *mother*, which should be /mʌðe/, as /mɔðə/ with the same vowel as in *bother*, /bɔðə/. For her, *done*, /dʌn/, and *don*, /dɔn/, are pronounced both as /dɔn/. This would not have happened if English had a standard five-vowel system.

10. Consonants. An ideal system of consonants consists of those found in most languages, and which adult learners find relatively easy—about twenty or so. Standard places of articulation involve the two lips, the tongue tip against the gums, and the back of the tongue against the soft palate at the rear of the mouth. These give voiceless stops (p, t, k), the corresponding voiced set (b, d, g), and corresponding sets of voiceless and voiced fricatives, and nasals. A single lateral (l) and some variety of rhotic, or r-sound, are pretty standard, as are semi-vowels y and w.

Beyond this, there are many kinds of luxuries—a retroflex series (with the tongue tip turned back) and secondary features of aspiration, palatalisation, labialisation, velarisation, pharyngealisation, glottalisation, and so on. All pose difficulties for adult learners and even for some native speakers. English apico-dental fricatives /θ/ as in *thin*, /θin/, and /ð/, as in *this*, /ðis/ (both written as *th*) are cross-linguistically unusual and frequently cause difficulty.

11. Syllable structure. The most common syllable type across the languages of the world is CV(C); sometimes the initial consonant is also optional, giving (C)V(C). This is the ideal structure, straightforward to process and to learn.

Some languages operate with a simpler template, just CV or (C)V. Others allow a proliferation of consonants at the beginning and at the end of a word. In Russian 'shake up' is *vstr'akhnut'* (where ' indicates the secondary feature of palatalisation). In some English dialects, *strengthens* is pronounced with an initial cluster of three consonants and a final one of four, /streŋθnz/. As a native speaker, I have always found the word sequence *Smith's crisps*, /smiθs krisps/, to be something of a tongue twister. Complex structures are a luxury, which may be of mixed benefit.

12. Tones. Every word consists of a sequence of vowels and consonants, and in pronouncing them the voice must adopt some level of pitch. Why not have contrasting pitch as well as contrasting vowels and consonants? There is nothing to lose and much to gain.

Tones can distinguish lexemes, and also mark grammatical categories, such as gender and tense. A tone choice may apply once for a word, or on every syllable within a word. See section 2.3.

The most common tone system has two members (generally high versus low), and this is the ideal size. Larger systems are a luxury and, of course, harder to master.

10.3 Grammar

13. Demonstratives. There may be just a two-term system of nominal demonstratives ('this', near speaker, and 'that', away from speaker) and corresponding adverbs ('here' and 'there'). The ideal is a three-term system, with a further contrast within 'that' between (i) 'that near addressee' and 'that distant from speaker and addressee', or (ii) 'that mid-distance' and 'that far', or (iii), in hilly country, 'that higher' and 'that lower than speaker'. A more extensive demonstrative system is a definite luxury.

14. Personal pronouns. The minimal acceptable system has separate forms for 1st, 2nd, and also 3rd person in singular and plural (here referring to more than one). A three-term number system is ideal, {singular, dual, plural (now referring to more than two)}. Larger number systems are, of course, useful but fall within the basket of luxuries.

Bound pronouns are not basic features for an ideal language, but they do engender succinctness. The one-word sentence in Warekena, *nu-wepa-pi* (1sgA-leave-2sgO) 'I am leaving you' was illustrated in section 2.5. It is better when bound pronouns are segmentable, as in Warekena, rather than irretrievably fused with other elements, as illustrated for Murinypata at the end of section 9.1.

15. Inclusive/exclusive. A basic feature of an ideal language is a distinction between inclusive (including addressee) and exclusive (excluding addressee) for non-singular 1st person pronouns. If, in English, John says to me *We've been invited to dinner with the boss*, I don't know whether 'we' means John and his wife (exclusive) or John and myself (inclusive). Not knowing can cause me embarrassment, which wouldn't happen if there were separate inclusive and exclusive forms of 'we'.

16. Anaphoric devices. There should be some way of integrating discourse by avoiding direct repetition of a noun or phrase which serves as topic for a sequence of clauses. This is typically achieved by use of 3rd person pronouns or demonstratives or both. For example, instead of

> I like to walk the dog because the dog is a friendly fellow and walking the dog is healthy exercise

one could say:

> I like to walk the dog because he is a friendly fellow and this is healthy exercise

Here pronoun *he* refers back to *the dog* and demonstrative *this* to *walking the dog*.

Languages vary in the anaphoric devices they have, but there should always be some.

17. Explicit marking of moods. For maximally efficient communication, there should be explicit marking (by something other than intonation; see feature 1 in section 10.1) to distinguish between a statement (declarative mood), a command (imperative mood), and a question (interrogative mood). One possibility is to leave declarative unmarked but to employ explicit affixes to indicate the other two moods. However, the ideal situation is to have overt marking for each mood, as illustrated for West Greenlandic Eskimo in section 3.1. West Greenlandic goes further, with different affixes for a polar question (expecting a 'yes'-or-'no'-type answer) and for a content question (expecting a substantive response). This is welcome, but not strictly necessary.

As outlined in section 3.1, some languages include several varieties of imperatives ('do here and now' versus 'do at some other time or place'). Imperatives relate to 2nd person in all languages, and in some are extended to 1st and 3rd person. There can be several kinds of polar interrogatives; for instance, expecting confirmation, or expressing surprise. All of these are useful but the number of such luxuries is limited, for each language, due simply to the limitations of the human brain.

18. Having a full set of content question words. An ideal language will have a separate form for each of the standard interrogative words: 'who', 'what', 'which', 'where', 'when', 'why', 'how', 'how much', and 'how many'. Note that English has separate forms for the first seven, but *how much* and *how many* are simply combinations of *how* plus an adjective: *How many cars are there?* is parallel to *How clever is she?* and to *How old is grandfather?*

As illustrated in section 3.1, an interrogative verb 'do what, do how' is most useful. It occurs in a relatively small number of languages (although widely scattered) and thus one hesitates to include it in the inventory for an ideal language.

19. Distinguishing between 'how much 'and 'how many'. Many languages have a single quantitative interrogative, 'how much/ how many' (section 3.1). If one hears, in such a language: 'That company owns lots of wells producing a huge amount of oil each month but I don't know exactly how much/many', it is unclear whether the interrogative is asking about the number of wells or the amount of oil. Many languages do have two words here, for instance *kìi* 'how many' and *thâwrày* 'how much' in Thai. This is clearly a desirable feature.

20. Having ample means of negating. Many languages with intricate word structures show negation just by an affix to the verb. Those with simpler word structures may have a separate negative word, and there can be wide possibilities for its placement. For example, in English one can say:

> Surely you couldn't have not known that he was not telling the truth

The *-n't* negates *you could have not known that* . . . ; the first *not* negates *have known that* . . . ; and the final *not* negates the complement clause *that he was telling the truth*.

There should be means for negating main clauses, every variety of subordinate clause, and also a noun phrase within a clause, as in English: *No sane person could believe that the world is flat.*

Most languages have forms 'no' and 'yes' as single word responses to a polar question. However, the discourse profile of others requires a full clause; a reply to 'Is she going?' would have to be 'She is going' or 'She is not going' (section 3.2). It is thus open to argument whether having a single-word negator 'no' is desirable for languages of every possible mien.

21. Possession. If there is a single possessive construction, the ideal situation is for there to be an explicit marker, rather than just possessor and possessee being placed in apposition. The marker can either go on the possessor (genitive) or on the possessee (pertensive): see section 3.3.

Many languages make a distinction between alienable possession (something that the possessor owns, and which they can sell) and inalienable possession (a part–whole relationship). The part can be material ('my foot') or abstract ('your name', 'Tom's smell', 'Henry's dream'). Kinship relations are sometimes coded as inalienable, sometimes as alienable, and sometimes split between the two.

Having several possessive constructions is most certainly a desirable feature.

22. Having a verb 'have'. Across the world, more languages lack a possessive verb, similar to English *have,* than include one. Whereas in English we say *I have a wife,* other languages might render this through constructions such as 'A wife is to me' or 'My wife exists'. Where there is a possessive verb, it is sometimes limited to ownership, or to ownership and kinship.

A verb of possession would be a useful component of an ideal language.

23. A system of case marking. If an activity involves two core participants, it is important to know which role each has; did Tom punch Fred, or did Fred punch Tom? (section 3.4). Some languages have no explicit mechanism, and the listener has to work it out—as best they can—from co-text and context. Obligatory bound pronouns can be a limited help. Using ordering of words is alright, but this takes away from word order the pragmatic possibilities it can embrace in a language with case marking.

The ideal technique, because it is clear and efficient, is a system of case inflections. The two main alternatives are of equal service. Either nominative case for A (transitive subject) and S (intransitive subject) versus accusative for O (transitive object). Or absolutive for O and S, opposed to ergative for A.

If a language has case affixes for distinguishing core participants, then there are generally a few further cases, perhaps half-a-dozen in all. One case (dative) may mark benefactive, another instrumental, with further cases for location 'at' or motion 'to' or 'from'. A medium-sized case system can be regarded as a basic feature; a larger one, with ten or twelve cases, is a luxury.

24. Copulas. Some languages show identity and attribution simply by juxtaposition, as in 'My mother a doctor' or 'That pig fat'. Ideally, these relationships are shown by a copula, which can be marked for tense and the like, in a similar fashion to transitive and intransitive verbs. (See section 3.5.)

Some languages have more than one copula; for instance, *be* and *become* in English. Others have distinct forms for positive and negative copulas. Both can be considered luxuries.

25. Techniques for linking clauses. For quite a number of languages, the only way of showing that two clauses are related is to juxtapose them within one intonation unit, something like 'John bought a car on Monday; it broke down the following day'. It is more effective to have an explicit marker of clause linking. In English, one could insert, between the two clauses just illustrated: *and*, just showing temporal sequence, or *but*, here indicating something unexpected.

An ideal language will have a range of clause linkers. Illustrating from English, they include cause (*John got fired because he was rude to the boss*), purpose (*Mary took the cat to town for it to be desexed*), and possible consequence (*Don't let the dog out in case it bites the mailman*). The disjunctive marker *or* can link words, or phrases, or clauses.

We sometimes find a linker which combines temporal ('when') and conditional ('if') meanings. The English sentences *When the rain stops, we'll have a picnic* and *If the rain stops, we'll have a picnic* would have identical translation in such a language. These two meanings should ideally be expressed by separate words.

26. Subordinate clauses. The ideal language will include a relative clause construction, one or more complement clause constructions, and a set of adverbial clause constructions (section 3.6).

A relative clause modifies a noun, in much the same way that an adjective does. One could say, in English, either *He is wearing [a red tie]* or *He is wearing [a tie [which is the colour of blood]]*. Some languages do have several kinds of relative clauses, perhaps relating to events which happen before or at the same time as the event of the main clause. This is a bit of a luxury.

A complement clause fills a core argument slot, as an alternative to a noun phrase. Many languages have what can be considered the ideal array of three varieties. In English, a Fact complement clause is marked by *that*, as in *I saw [that John and Tom were fighting]$_O$*, an Activity clause is marked by *-ing*, as in *Mary enjoys [going to the theatre]$_O$*, and a Potentiality clause is marked by *to*, as in *I want [to eat a mango]$_O$*. (With a plain noun phrase in place of the complement clause, we could have *I saw [the fight]$_O$*, *Mary enjoys [plays]$_O$*, and *I want [a mango]$_O$*.)

Some languages have just one complement clause construction, which may cover all three meanings. Others verge on luxury

231

with more then three types; for example, a distinction may be made between direct and indirect potentiality/purpose.

An adverbial subordinate clause is an alternative to a plain adverb. They typically refer to time, as in *We'll wash the dishes [after the guests have gone]*, and to place, as in *You'll find it [where you left it]*. There may also be adverbial phrases—of time, as in *They'll come [in the morning]*, of place, as in *The President lives [in the White House]*, and also of manner, as in *She cooked it [in the old familiar way]*. These are all most useful construction types.

27. Pivots and switch-reference. If two clauses share an argument, which is in a specified function in each, then a pivot condition may allow it to be omitted from the second clause with no loss of meaning (section 3.6).

Consider the following coordination of a transitive and an intransitive clause, where the S argument is omitted from the second clause:

(1)   John$_A$ saw Mary$_O$ (and) —$_S$ ran away

English operates with an S/A pivot. If two coordinated clauses share an argument and it is in S or A function in each clause, then it can be omitted from the second clause. For English, sentence (1) states that it was John who ran away.

The alternative is an S/O pivot, as in Dyirbal—if two coordinated clauses share an argument and it is in S or O function in each clause, then it can be omitted from the second clause. When (1) is expressed in Dyirbal, it states that it was Mary who ran away. The omitted S argument of the second cause is taken to be identical with the O argument of the first clause.

Having a pivot condition—of either variety—facilitates succinct discourse. Many languages lack any pivot, with the result that hearing a sentence such as (1), it is not clear who it was that ran away. Extra information would be needed to clarify this.

A number of languages have what is effectively an alternative to a pivot condition—switch-reference marking (section 3.6). The verb in the first clause of (1) would be marked either for 'same subject', which would mean that it was John who ran away, or for 'different subject', which would imply that it was Mary who ran away. (Note that in some languages switch-reference marking goes on the verb of the first clause, in others on the verb of the second clause.)

An ideal language should have either a pivot condition or switch-reference marking.

28. Genders and classifiers. A system of genders fulfils semantic and grammatical roles. It provides a partial codification of the way in which a society views and categorises its life-style and environment. Gender plays a useful role in anaphora. And if an adjective agrees in gender with the noun it modifies, the noun may be omitted with some indication of its reference being retained in the adjective. For example, *bona*, the feminine nominative form of 'good' in Latin, can be used without a noun and indicates something good of feminine gender. In contrast, *good* in English includes no such information (and indeed, requires a following noun in most circumstances).

A basic component of an ideal language is a gender system of three terms, two of which relate (among other things) to female and male humans. Larger systems are a luxury (and each language can only handle a limited number of luxuries). English does not have a gender system, as the term is used here (section 4.1). But its sex-based 3rd person pronouns (with occasional extensions beyond humankind) are a useful second-best, with a strong anaphoric role.

Some languages include a set of classifiers, which may have a wider semantic role than genders but lack their grammatical possibilities.

29. Definiteness. Although found, in explicit form, in a minority of languages, a definite/indefinite distinction is so useful that it should be considered basic (section 4.2). If one hears *Max was the founder of the firm*, it is clear that he did it all by himself, whereas *Max was a founder of the firm* states that he was one of several people involved. A language lacking definite/indefinite articles would just have 'Max was founder of firm', which is vague.

30. Tenses and modalities. All languages make explicit reference to place, but some are vague with respect to time. An ideal language has at least a basic tense system; it may distinguish past from present from future. However, past and present are known, whereas what has not yet happened can only be seen in terms of prediction, obligation, necessity, possibility, desire, and so on (section 4.3). An alternative to having a future tense is a system of modalities, dealing with features such as those just listed.

Some languages have several past tenses, and a few have several futures. However, the ways in which they divide up time vary considerably. These fall under the heading of luxury, as do various varieties of aspect, and the like.

31. Evidentiality. People who don't have it in their languages often wish they did—an obligatory grammatical system whereby *how* a speaker knows a certain thing must be specified. The nature of the evidence has to be stated (section 4.4). Was the speaker just told about it, or did they see it for themself, or know about it in some other way?

Around a quarter of the world's languages include such a system—of varying sizes—in their grammar. One of the basics for an ideal language should be an evidentiality system of modest size, with perhaps three or so terms.

32. Comparative constructions. In section 4.5 it was noted that many small egalitarian societies do not think in terms of competitiveness between people. They have no need for lexemes such as 'win' and 'lose', or for a comparative construction in their grammar.

In larger societies, competition is the name of the game: 'Mary performed better than John in the exam, and so landed the job'. Not all the languages of such peoples include an explicit comparative construction in their grammar, but this must be a basic component of an ideal language.

The most common construction type is of the pattern: 'My daughter is more intelligent than your son', where 'your son' is the standard of comparison, 'my daughter' is what is being compared against it (the comparee), 'intelligent' is the parameter, and 'more' the index of comparison. However, other schemes can be equally effective; for example, 'My daughter exceeds your son in intelligence'.

Generally, two people or things are compared in terms of a quality. There may be luxurious extensions, such as comparing two qualities with respect to a person, as in the English *Jane is more stupid than rude*.

33. Passive constructions. In a language like English, some transitive verbs may either include or omit an object (O) noun phrase; for example, *Tom has been painting (the garage) all morning*, and *Ruth sang (Jerusalem) in church yesterday*. However, a transitive subject (A) cannot be directly omitted. What has to be done is apply a passive derivation:

[A thug]$_A$ attacked Mary$_O$ → Mary$_S$ was attacked (by a thug)

The original O argument, *Mary*, goes into S function in the passive (which is intransitive). The original A argument, *a thug*, can be included at the end, marked with *by*, but is most often omitted.

There are many uses for a passive such as *Mary was attacked*. It may be employed if the speaker does not know who the attacker was, or does know and prefers not to reveal their identity, or just to focus on the result of the activity (section 4.6). Or to meet an S/A pivot condition in discourse (see feature 27), as in *Mary$_S$ walked home alone after dark and—$_S$ was attacked*.

The various roles for a passive make it a desirable feature for an ideal language.

34. Reflexive and reciprocal constructions. In all societies, people do things to themselves. Some languages have no special way of describing this. Saying 'I cut me' is clear enough, but if one hears 'Betty cut her', this is ambiguous between 'her' referring to Betty or to someone else.

Other languages have an explicit reflexive construction, of which there are two main types. These are equally effective, and an ideal language could include either. The first alternative maintains the clause as transitive and places a reflexive pronoun into the O slot; for example, *Mary$_A$ cut herself$_O$* in English. The other technique creates an intransitive clause, with the protagonist in

S function and the verb bearing a reflexive derivational affix: 'Mary$_S$ cut-REFLEXIVE'. This is illustrated in section 4.6.

Turning now to reciprocals, there are languages in which one can only say 'John punched Tom and Tom punched John'. However, most do have a reciprocal construction, with the same two possibilities as reflexives. That is, there may be a reciprocal pronoun, as in English *[John and Tom]$_A$ punched [each other/one another]$_O$*, or a reciprocal derivational suffix to the verb, '[John and Tom]$_S$ punched-RECIPROCAL'.

Reflexive and reciprocal are generally marked differently but occasionally in the same way. The latter would be avoided in an ideal language.

35. Causatives. Every language has intransitive clauses describing activities and states. And there is generally a grammatical technique deriving a transitive clause specifying who was responsible for the activity or state. Some languages have a causative affix to the verb. In Jarawara, we can start with an intransitive clause:

[hajo   ati]$_S$ saiha
radio   voice   be.audible
'The radio's voice is audible (that is, the radio is turned on)'

To the verb can be added causative prefix *na-*:

[hajo   ati]$_O$ o-na-saiha
radio   voice   1sgA-CAUSATIVE-be.audible
'I made the radio's voice be audible (that is, I turned the radio on)'

The original S argument of the intransitive (here *hajo ati* 'radio's voice') goes into O function in the transitive causative. And a new argument is introduced, the causer, here 1st person singular, 'I', shown by prefix *o-* to the verb.

Languages with simpler word structure tend to use periphrastic constructions, with a separate word 'make'. For example, corresponding to *Judy cleaned her room* in English we get the causative *Mother made Judy clean her room*. In some languages causatives are only based on intransitive verbs; in others they may also apply to some or to many transitives.

Almost all—but probably not quite all—languages have causative constructions of one type or another; this should be a basic feature of an ideal language. Sometimes there are two causatives, with quite different meanings, a number of which were illustrated in section 4.7. These are a welcome luxury.

Section 4.7 also described applicative constructions, in which the S argument of an intransitive becomes A of a transitive applicative (generally marked by an applicative affix to the verb), and what was a peripheral argument is taken into the core, in O function. From 'Father$_S$ lives in Bilyana (with uncle)' may be derived 'Father$_A$ lives-APPLICATIVE uncle$_O$ in Bilyana', literally 'Father lives-with uncle in Bilyana'. Applicatives are useful for focusing on what is now the O argument, which can feed pivot conditions and facilitate discourse organisation generally. Applicative constructions are found in around one quarter of the world's languages. They probably do not quite qualify as a basic feature.

10.4 Vocabulary

We can begin with a number of general features.

36. It is best to have a minimum of double duty words. When a lexeme belongs to two word classes (for example, both noun and verb) this carries the possibility of sentences being ambiguous (see sections 2.6 and 7.2). Consider the newspaper headline:

French bridge splits

The most obvious interpretation of this is that a structure with a road on top, over a river or whatever, somewhere in France, has divided into several parts. However, on reading the report it becomes clear that this is a political rather than a material matter. There was a rift between two factions at an economic summit, and the French delegation sought to establish a common cause between them.

This ambiguity is due to each of the three words undertaking double duty:

- *French* is an adjective in the first interpretation and a noun in the second.
- *Bridge* is a noun in the first and a verb (with metaphoric meaning) in the second.
- *Splits* is a verb in the first, a noun in the second.

If there had been newspaper headlines in Old English times, no such ambiguity would have been encountered. This was because there was very little double duty in Old English. For example, the noun and verb corresponding to present-day *bridge* had different forms: *brycg* and *brycgian* respectively. Word structures were simplified as the language developed, leading to double duty and unwelcome ambiguity.

37. Simple lexemes are preferable to descriptive labels. For example, rather than having a word 'blue', a language might just use 'sky-coloured'. This does make it a little tricky to remark: 'The sky is not blue today'.

A sweet fruit of the genus *Actinidia*, which originated in China, came to be cultivated in New Zealand. It was first marketed as *Chinese gooseberry* but didn't sell; nobody liked this long name. Then someone thought of relabelling it as *Kiwifruit*, typically shortened to *Kiwi*. It became an immense success.

When a new foodstuff was introduced from the Americas, the French dubbed it *pomme de terre*, 'apple of the earth', and this cute designation—relating a vegetable to a fruit—has been retained. *Potato* is less fancy but simpler.

38. Having a goodly array of abstract nouns. Surely no one would deny that it is beneficial to have a set of abstract nouns such as 'time', 'colour', 'size', and 'age' (section 7.4). They enable us to ask 'What time is it?' rather than 'Where is the sun in the sky?', and 'What colour is it?' rather than 'Is it red, or green, or blue, or yellow or what?'

39. Distinguishing process from result. After a process of covering has been applied to some object, it can be described—using the past participle of the verb—as 'covered'. However, there are different ways of being covered—with a blanket too thick or too skimpy or just right, fully or partially, and so on. Dyirbal has adjective *ngulguñ* (quite separate from verb *dadil* 'cover') meaning 'covered in just the right manner'. And similarly with other result adjectives; see section 7.4. This is plainly an advantageous feature.

We can now turn to some more specific features.

40. All kinds of names. In an ideal language, every person has a different name, and these contain useful information; for instance, including the first name of the father, as in Russian, or the last name of the mother, as in Spanish and Portuguese (section 9.2).

Labels for social roles should be unambiguous; for example, a distinction is needed between 'queen' as ruler, and 'queen' as wife of a male ruler (section 7.1).

41. Kin terms. Much confusion is avoided by having separate terms for distinct classes of relative. For example, not lumping together 'father's mother' and 'mother's mother' as just 'grand-mother'. And actually having a term for 'son or daughter's mother-in-law', similar to 'co-mother-in-law' in Indian English (section 7.1). Speakers of other varieties of English simply don't know what to call such a relative, and frequently fret over it.

42. General vocabulary. Each language deals with a set of universal concepts—things, qualities, states, activities—but these will not have identical ranges of meaning. For example, one language has separate lexemes for 'lower arm', 'wrist', and 'hand', while another has a single lexeme covering all three.

It is not practical to work in terms of itemised features, checking off each one for every language, as was done for phonology and grammar. General vocabulary is best compared directly between two languages, examining in turn each semantic field—verbs of motion, verbs of thinking, verbs of speaking; physical property adjectives, value adjectives; nouns for flora, for fauna, for celestial objects; and so on. These will involve detailed matching of corresponding lexemes, a task which will be time-consuming and also fascinating.

For example, one language has two lexemes 'meet as planned' and 'meet by chance', whereas English has a single verb. On hearing *John met Mary at the station*, one does not know whether it was a pre-arranged meeting or an accidental encounter. The other language scores higher than English for this feature, but no doubt the situation would be reversed for other points.

In addition to the universal ideas, each language also has a stack of lexemes relating to its speakers' life-style, economic system, social organisation, and environment. These can only sensibly be compared where there is considerable similarity of cultures—for example, between two languages from developed countries in Europe, or two from the Sepik swamps of New Guinea, or two from the Amazonian jungle.

10.5 Envoi

The inventory of features listed in previous sections should not be regarded as a blueprint for fabricating a 'model language'. To link together each of the 'desirable' features discussed here would produce something of a hotch-potch.

A language is a social organism, a living thing, that responds to the environment which it inhabits. Each language has its own character, which has evolved steadily over time. It mirrors the society that it serves, gradually shifting its profile in association with cultural changes, forces within itself, and contact with other languages and cultures. A language has its own 'genius', as it were, something which can be felt, but scarcely made fully explicit.

A language serves its own purposes, but does each language serve the purposes equally well? I have sought here to articulate this question. There are recurrent similarities across all human societies, functions that must be fulfilled, communicative needs to be met. Addressing the forty-two features identified here provides an assessment of how well a language fares, in certain ways.

Humankind is distinguished from other creatures by its adaptability. The same applies for human languages. A speaker must have the means to be fully explicit when required, but purposefully vague when this is socially appropriate. There must always be a balance between economy of expression and clarity of meaning. Cohesiveness in discourse organisation may be relaxed for rhetorical effect, when repetition serves to drive home a position. Every lexeme and every grammatical element has a central ('literal') meaning, but it is the additional nuances, and subtle semantic contrasts, which provide colour and vivacity.

We can now engage with the main question, set out in the title of this book.

Chapter 11
Facing up to the question

Can one language be considered better than another? It is up to you, the reader, to decide. Proceed as follows.

(a) Assess the basic features for an ideal language, as set out in the previous chapter. Adapt them to suit your own judgement, perhaps adding more features and deleting some.

(b) Plainly, not all features are of equal importance; they need to be weighted. For instance, Subordinate Clauses (feature 26)—which includes relative clauses, complement clauses, and adverbial clauses—clearly needs to be weighted more heavily than Comparative Constructions (feature 32). Opinions will vary concerning the appropriate weighting for General Vocabulary (feature 42). Should it be reckoned to be worth a quarter as much as all phonological and grammatical features combined? Or more?

People will vary in weightings according to their major concerns—as they are most interested in learning and teaching, or in translation, or in aesthetics, or in argumentation and inference, and so on.

Are Some Languages Better than Others? First Edition. R. M. W. Dixon.

(c) Take two languages for each of which you have reasonable facility in understanding and speaking (plus reading and writing, if that is appropriate). You should also—and this is important—have a good understanding of the linguistic structure of each language.

Check off each language against the weighted list or basic features, as amended by you.

(d) Compare the 'scores' for the two languages, and there you have it.

This book is, in essence, speculation—a hypothesis awaiting confirmation. Suppose that you apply the criteria set out in the previous chapter (suitably modified and weighted, to suit your predilections) and decide that language B is better—probably only slightly better—than language W.

What should this imply? Presumably some—preferably most, probably not all—of the following. That B is more easily under-stood by a listener. That it is more straightforward for description by a linguist, and for the preparation of teaching materials by an applied linguist. That it requires less effort to be acquired as L2 by an adult. That it poses relatively little difficulty when being translated out of, or being translated into. That it provides greater specificity for naming, and for describing social stratification. That it has richer resources for expressing emotions. That it is highly suitable for enabling cooperative endeavour, for conveying information in a succinct and memorisable manner, for func-tioning as a vehicle for aesthetic expression, for being a conduit for scientific thought and argumentation. That it is effective for mass persuasion. And no doubt more besides.

Let's check it out.

Notes and sources

As mentioned in the preface, I have tried to keep the use of technical terms to a minimum. Terms which I found could be done without (in the present context) include, among others: morphology, morpheme, allophone, clitic, constituent, valency. Linguistic topics which have not been included, within the short scope of the present volume, include: noun incorporation, serial verb constructions, the realis/irrealis distinction, markedness, neutralisation, logophoricity, ideophones (this is far from an exhaustive list).

Many examples are drawn from those languages I know best, from four decades of immersion fieldwork—Dyirbal (1972 and 2015 publications) and Yidiñ (1977) from North Queensland, Jarawara from Amazonia (2004), and the Boumaa dialect of Fijian (1988). I have freely drawn on my earlier publications, especially the three-volume *Basic linguistic theory* (2010–12). Indications are given below concerning detailed treatment of topics in *BLT*. Readers who have enjoyed the present work could go on to a fuller—but still user-friendly—statement of the main principles of linguistics in Alexandra Y. Aikhenvald's *The art of grammar: A practical guide* (2014).

Fieldwork anecdotes are scattered through this volume. Anyone wanting more could go to the account of my adventures in Australia, *Searching for Aboriginal languages: Memoirs of a fieldworker* (1984, 1989, 2011), and to my academic autobiography *I am a linguist* (2011).

Chapter 1

1.4 The finest essay on the detrimental effects of writing is 'The bugbear of literacy', chapter II (pp. 19–35) of Coomaraswamy

(1943), from which the quotations in this section are taken. Plato in *Phaedrus* 275. Kittredge quote from his introduction to F. J. Child's *The English and Scottish popular ballads.*

1.5 Recent discussions of 'complexity' include McWhorter (2001) and Sampson, Gil, and Trudgill (2009).

1.6 Quote from James Boswell's *Life of Johnson*, entry for Wednesday 13 May 1778. A full account of the Dyirbal kinship system is in chapter 4 of Dixon (2015).

Chapter 2

Hua from Haiman (1980: 258). There is further information on languages with 'up'/'down' demonstratives in Dixon (2010b: 242–3). Information on the Pennsylvania German language spoken by Old Order Mennonites is from Burridge (2002).

2.3 For rising intonation in questions see Dixon (2012: 394–5). Data on Maale from Amha (2001: 28), on Dhaasanac from Tosco (2001: 73), on Fur from Waag (2010: 45). Quote from Chao (1976: 88).

2.4 Data on Alamblak from Bruce (1984: 161), on Warao from Osborn (1967: 46–9), on Manambu from Alexandra Y. Aikhenvald, private communication (and see 2008: 290–2), on Crow from Graczyk (2007: 141).

Verbalising suffix *-en* in English is (roughly) added to adjectives referring to dimension and physical property, which end in *p, t, d, k, f, th, s,* and *sh*. Fuller details are in Dixon (2014: 175–8).

2.5 Detailed discussion of demonstrative and pronoun systems is in Dixon (2010b: 189–261). Old English also had dual 1st and 2nd person pronouns; see, for instance, Quirk and Wrenn (1957: 38). Warekena data from Alexandra Y. Aikhenvald, personal communication (and see 1998: 293).

2.6 Halpern (1942) describes kin terms as verbs in Yuman languages.

Chapter 3

Indonesian has just a few masculine/feminine pairs (such as *suami* 'husband', *isteri* 'wife'). Beyond these, masculine *laki-laki* or *lelaki* and feminine *perempuan* are added after nouns with human reference (for example, *adik* 'younger sibling') while masculine *djantan* and feminine *betina* are added after a noun referring to a non-human animate (*singa* 'lion', and so on); see Kwee (1965: 55). For Cantonese see Matthews and Yip (1994: 189–92, 198–9).

3.1 Information on West Greenlandic from Sadock (1984) and Fortescue (1984: 23–4, 287–91); on Mupun from Frajzyngier 1993: 359–66); on Abun from Berry and Berry (1999: 109). There are fuller discussions of commands and imperatives in Aikhenvald (2010), and of questions and interrogatives in Dixon (2012: 376–433).

3.2 Information on Tariana from Aikhenvald (2003: 122, 177, 400–8); on Somali from Saeed (1993: 234, 248); on Newar from Hale and Shrestha (2006: 185–6). There is a fuller discussion of negation in Dixon (2012: 89–137).

3.3 Information on Angami from Giridhar (1980: 48); on Acehnese from Durie (1985: 109–10); on Mandarin from Li and Thompson (1981: 113–40); on Karbi from Jeyapaul (1987: 78); on Amele from Roberts (1987: 137–40); on Lango from Noonan (1992: 77–83, 156–9). There is a fuller discussion of possession in Dixon (2010b: 262–312).

3.4 Enfield (2007: 272–7) provides a revealing account of core argument identification in Lao, a language lacking cases, bound pronouns, and strict ordering of elements within a clause.

3.5 For Hungarian see Kenesei, Vago, and Fenyvesi (1998: 58–62). There is a fuller discussion of copula clauses and verbless clauses in Dixon (2010b: 159–88).

3.6 Information on Chickasaw from Payne (1980: 89–90). For fuller information on clause linking see Dixon (2009); on relative clause constructions and complementation see Dixon (2010b: 313–421).

Chapter 4

4.1 Information of Swahili based on Ashton (1947) and Loogman (1965); on Thai from Iwasaki and Ingkaphirom (2005: 76–8); on Malto from Mahapatra (1979: 61–2, 76–7, 121–40). A detailed description of classifiers in Yidiñ is in Dixon (1977: 480–96; 1982: 185–205; 2015: chapter 3). There is a fuller discussion of gender and classifiers in Aikhenvald (2000).

4.2 Note that earlier writings on Dyirbal referred to the 'articles' as 'noun markers'.

4.3 Information on Bini from Dunn (1968: 216–17, 97–8, 123–5); on Washo from Mithun (1999: 152–3) based on Jacobsen (1964: 589–647); on Tagalog from Schachter and Otanes (1972: 66–9). For fuller information on tense, modality, aspect, and other verbal categories see Dixon (2012: 1–44).

4.4 There is full discussion—and ample exemplification—of evidentiality systems in Aikhenvald (2004).

4.5 There is a comprehensive account of comparative constructions in Dixon (2012: 343–75).

4.6 Information on Guugu Yimidhirr from Haviland (1979: 119–26, 60–1). For fuller information on reflexives, reciprocals, passives, and antipassives see Dixon (2012: 138–238).

4.7 Information on Amharic from Amberber (2000: 319); on Hindi from Kachru (1976) and Saksena (1982); on Kammu from Svantesson (1983: 103–11); on Javanese from Suhandano (2015: 50–62). For fuller information on causatives and applicatives see Dixon (2012: 239–375).

Chapter 5

5.2 Information on Kyaka Enga from Draper and Draper (2002: 134, 238). There is a useful cross-linguistic survey of suppletive forms for 'give' in Comrie (2003).

There is another variety of useful suppletion, whereby a verb has different forms depending on the number of referents of the S (intransitive subject) or of the O (transitive object) argument. For instance, intransitive verb 'fall to the ground' in Jarawara is *-sona-* if just one thing is falling, and *foro -na-* if more than one thing. Transitive verb 'throw' is *koro -na-* if one thing is thrown, and *were -na-* if more than one thing. A cross-linguistic survey of this phenomenon is in Dixon (2012: 62–5).

5.3 Information on Kugu Nganhcara from Smith and Johnson (2000: 421–2).

Chapter 6

6.3 Quotation from Meillet (1970: 62). Full discussion of the Vaupés River Basin as a linguistic area is in Aikhenvald (1996, 2002). Bridging constructions have also been termed 'tail–head linkage' and 'head–tail linkage'. Information on Tariana from Aikhenvald (2003: 577–81, 6–8, 257–323, and personal communication). There is a comprehensive discussion of contact situations in Trudgill (2011). Information on the histories of *goose/geese* and *mouse/mice* from Watkins (1985: 21, 43). Quotation from McWhorter (2001: 125). For Pirahã, see Aikhenvald and Dixon (1999), and further references therein.

Chapter 7

7   Information on Nuer from Evans-Pritchard (1940: 41–4). Payne (2003) is a useful account of colour and pattern designations for cattle in Maa, another East African language. For Nyawaygi see Dixon (1983: 516). Information on Manambu and Yalaku from Aikhenvald (2009 and personal communication).

7.5 Information on vocabulary sizes of Shakespeare and Milton from Jespersen (1922: 126); on word frequencies in the Cobuild dictionary from Sinclair (2001: xlii). For Basic English see, among other sources, Ogden (1932), a book written in Basic.

Chapter 8

8   For example, Jakobson (1971: 492) stated: 'Thus the true difference between languages is not in what may or may not be expressed but in what must or must not be conveyed by the speaker.'

8.1 Examples of temporal-type adverbs are taken from Cantonese (Matthews and Yip 1994: 178–228). Sources for information on causatives in Hindi and Kammu were given under section 4.7. For Japanese see Shibatani (1990: 309), Tonoike (1978), and Tsujimura (1996: 247–9), and for Cavineña see Guillaume (2008: 287–306) and Guillaume and Rose (2010: 388–9).

8.3 The seminal discussion of diglossia is Ferguson (1959).

Chapter 9

9.1 Information on Yanyuwa from Kirton (1971: 28); on Murinypata from Walsh (2012: 368–8).

9.2 Harrison's (1990) *Stealing people's names* describes naming practices in the Sepik. Warlpiri quote from Meggitt (1962: 278–9). Quote from Elkin (1954: 178–9).

9.3 Information on classifiers in Thai from Haas (1942) and Carpenter (1991).

9.4 Quotation from Bergman (1970: 91). Information on 'what I miss' from Angeliki Alvanoudi (Greek), Valérie Guérin (French), Elena Mihas (Russian), Azeb Amha (Amharic and Wolaitta), and Katarzyna Wojtylak (Polish).

Chapter 10

10.1 For differences between American and British vowels, see Wells (1982: 122–4). Data on Indonesian from Sneddon (1996: 16–17). Quote concerning Spanish from Butt and Benjamin (2004: 551).

English does have ways of forming diminutive/endearing forms of some nouns (which have an appropriate phonological form). One can say *doggy, dogsy, doggy-woggy, dogsy-wogsy*. And, with a person's name: *Katey, Katsy, Katy-waty, Katsy-watsy* (see Dixon 2014: 171–7). However, this is used only a little, in restricted registers, whereas diminutives and augmentatives in languages such as Spanish and Polish have wide use in every variety of the language.

10.3 Thai interrogatives from Iwasaki and Ingkaphirom (2005: 291). Jarkey (2006) describes five varieties of complement clause constructions for White Hmong, including two Fact constructions (used with different types of verb), one Activity, and direct and indirect Purpose.

Abbreviations

Introduced in section 2.2:

C	consonant
V	vowel

Introduced in section 3.4, terms for core arguments of a predicate:

S   intransitive subject function, such as *Mary* in *Mary$_S$ laughed*

A   transitive subject function, such as *John* in *John$_A$ hit Tom$_O$*; the participant who initiates and/or controls the activity

O   transitive object function, such as *Tom* in *John$_A$ hit Tom$_O$*; the other core participant in a transitive clause which may be affected by the activity

Introduced in section 3.5:

CS   copula subject, such as *the teacher* in [*The teacher*]$_{CS}$ *is clever$_{CC}$*.

CC   copula complement, such as *clever* in [*The teacher*]$_{CS}$ *is clever$_{CC}$*.

Introduced in section 5.1:

*   marking a form reconstructed for a putative ancestor (a proto-language)

Introduced in section 9.3:

L1   first (or native) language, learnt naturally as a child

L2   second language, a non-native language, learnt after the first language

Abbreviations

In examples from Jarawara (sections 2.1, 6.1, 6.2):

IP	immediate past tense
e	eyewitness evidentiality
f	feminine
AUX	auxiliary verb
DEC	declarative mood
n	non-eyewitness evidentiality
m	masculine
REDUP	reduplication

Phonological representations of the pronunciation of words in English are shown within slant brackets; for instance *through* is /θruː/.

Acknowledgements

My first and greatest debt is to those indigenous linguists who have shared with me the joy of their languages—recording, teaching, correcting, approving, and always encouraging. Their friendship and dedication were a constant source of inspiration. Deserving of particular mention are Chloe Grant, George Watson, Bessie Jerry, Mollie Raymond, and Ida Henry for Dyirbal; Dick Moses, Tilly Fuller, and George Davis for Yidiñ, Willie Seaton for Nyawaygi (all in Australia); Josefa Cookanacagi and Inoke Soqooviti for the Boumaa dialect of Fijian; and Okomobi, Mioto, Soki, Botenawaa, and Kamo for Jarawara in Brazil.

At an early stage of working on this project, many friends and colleagues offered encouragement (and a few heated discouragement). I am grateful for the useful comments provided in 1989 by Paul Hopper, Neil Tennant, and Peter Trudgill; and in 1991 by Dell Hymes and—most especially—Robbins Burling. Alexandra Aikhenvald provided feedback in 1994 on an early version and then, in 2014, insightful and inspiring comments on the final thing. Also in 2014, Hannah Sarvasy pointed out errors and provided cogent suggestions.

A further thanks to friends who responded to my enquiry concerning what they missed from their L1 when speaking English (section 9.4): Azeb Amha, Angeliki Alvanoudi, Valérie Guérin, Elena Mihas, and Katarzyna Wojtylak.

Canberra, April 1989—
Cairns, June 2015

References

Aikhenvald, Alexandra Y. 1996. 'Areal linguistics in north-west Amazonia', *Anthropological Linguistics* 38: 73–116.

Aikhenvald, Alexandra Y. 1998. 'Warekena', pp. 225–439 of *Handbook of Amazonian languages*, Vol. 4, edited by Desmond C. Derbyshire and Geoffrey K. Pullum. Berlin: Mouton de Gruyter.

Aikhenvald, Alexandra Y. 2000. *Classifiers: A typology of noun categorization devices*. Oxford: Oxford University Press.

Aikhenvald, Alexandra Y. 2002. *Language contact in Amazonia*. Oxford: Oxford University Press.

Aikhenvald, Alexandra Y. 2003. *A grammar of Tariana, from north-west Amazonia*. Cambridge: Cambridge University Press.

Aikhenvald, Alexandra Y. 2004. *Evidentiality*. Oxford: Oxford University Press.

Aikhenvald, Alexandra Y. 2008. *The Manambu language of East Sepik, Papua New Guinea*. Oxford: Oxford University Press.

Aikhenvald, Alexandra Y. 2009. '"Eating", "drinking" and "smoking": A generic verb and its semantics in Manambu', pp. 91–108 of *The linguistics of eating and drinking*, edited by John Newman. Amsterdam: John Benjamins.

Aikhenvald, Alexandra Y. 2010. *Imperatives and commands*. Oxford: Oxford University Press.

Aikhenvald, Alexandra Y. 2014. *The art of grammar: A practical guide*. Oxford: Oxford University Press.

Aikhenvald, Alexandra Y. and Dixon, R. M. W. 1999. 'Other small families and isolates', pp. 341–84 of *The Amazonian languages*, edited by R. M. W. Dixon and Alexandra Y. Aikhenvald. Cambridge: Cambridge University Press.

Amberber, Mengistu. 2000. 'Valency-changing and valency-encoding devices in Amharic', pp. 312–32 of *Changing valency: Case studies in transitivity*, edited by R. M. W. Dixon and Alexandra Y. Aikhenvald. Cambridge: Cambridge University Press.

Amha, Azeb. 2001. *The Maale language*. Leiden: CNWS, University of Leiden.

Archer, W. G. 1943. 'The heron will not twist his moustache', *Journal of the Bihar and Orissa Research Society* 29: 5–73.

Ashton, E. O. 1947. *Swahili grammar (including intonation)*. 2nd edition. London: Longmans.

Bergman, Ingmar. 1970. *Wild strawberries*, translated by Lars Malmström and David Kushner. London: Lorimer.

Berry, Keith and Christine. 1999. *A description of Abun, a West Papuan language of Irian Jaya*. Canberra: Pacific Linguistics.

Bruce, Les. 1984. *The Alamblak language of Papua New Guinea (East Sepik)*. Canberra: Pacific Linguistics.

Burridge, Kate. 2002. 'Changes within Pennsylvania German grammar', pp. 207–32 of *Ethnosyntax: Explorations in grammar and culture*, edited by N. J. Enfield. Oxford: Oxford University Press.

Butt, John and Benjamin, Carmen. 2004. *A new reference grammar of Modern Spanish*. 4th edition. London: Hodder Arnold.

Carpenter, Kathie. 1991. 'Later rather than sooner: Extralinguistic categories in the acquisition of Thai classifiers', *Journal of Child Language* 18: 93–113.

Chao, Yuen Ren. 1976. 'Chinese as symbolic system', pp. 84–96 of *Aspects of Chinese sociolinguistics: Essays by Yuen Ren Chao*, selected and introduced by Anwar S. Dil. Stanford, Calif.: Stanford University Press. [Paper first published in 1973.]

Comrie, Bernard. 2003. 'Recipient person suppletion in the verb "give"', pp. 265–81 of *Language and life: Essays in memory of Kenneth L. Pike*, edited by Mary Ruth Wise, Thomas N. Headland, and Ruth M. Brend. Dallas: SIL International and University of Texas at Arlington.

References

Coomaraswamy, Ananda K. 1943. *Am I my brother's keeper?* New York: John Day.

Dixon, R. M. W. 1972. *The Dyirbal language of North Queensland.* Cambridge: Cambridge University Press.

Dixon, R. M. W. 1977. *A grammar of Yidiɲ.* Cambridge: Cambridge University Press.

Dixon, R. M. W. 1982. *Where have all the adjectives gone? And other essays in semantics and syntax.* Berlin: Mouton.

Dixon, R. M. W. 1983. 'Nyawaygi', pp. 430–525 of *Handbook of Australian languages*, Vol. 3, edited by R. M. W. Dixon and Barry J. Blake. Canberra: The Australian National University Press, and Amsterdam: John Benjamins.

Dixon, R. M. W. 1984. *Searching for Aboriginal languages: Memoirs of a fieldworker.* St Lucia: University of Queensland Press. Reissued in 1989 by The University of Chicago Press, and in 2011 by Cambridge University Press.

Dixon, R. M. W. 1988. *A grammar of Boumaa Fijian.* Chicago: University of Chicago Press.

Dixon, R. M. W. 2004. *The Jarawara language of southern Amazonia.* Oxford: Oxford University Press.

Dixon, R. M. W. 2009. 'The semantics of clause linking in typological perspective', pp. 1–55 of *The semantics of clause linking: A cross-linguistic typology*, edited by R. M. W. Dixon and Alexandra Y. Aikhenvald. Oxford: Oxford University Press.

Dixon, R. M. W. 2010a. *Basic linguistic theory*, Vol. 1, *Methodology.* Oxford: Oxford University Press.

Dixon, R. M. W. 2010b. *Basic linguistic theory*, Vol. 2, *Grammatical topics.* Oxford: Oxford University Press.

Dixon, R. M. W. 2011. *I am a linguist.* Leiden: Brill.

Dixon, R. M. W. 2012. *Basic linguistic theory*, Vol. 3, *Further grammatical topics.* Oxford: Oxford University Press.

Dixon, R. M. W. 2014. *Making new words: Morphological derivation in English.* Oxford: Oxford University Press.

Dixon, R. M. W. 2015. *Edible gender, mother-in-law style, and other grammatical wonders: Studies in Dyirbal, Yidiñ and Warrgamay.* Oxford: Oxford University Press.

Draper, Norm and Sheila. 2002. *Dictionary of Kyaka Enga, Papua New Guinea.* Canberra: Pacific Linguistics.

Dunn, Ernest F. 1968. *An introduction to Bini.* East Lansing, Mich.: Michigan State University, African Studies Center.

Durie, Mark. 1985. *A grammar of Acehnese, on the basis of a dialect of North Aceh.* Dordrecht: Foris.

Elkin, A. P. 1954. *The Australian Aborigines: How to understand them.* 3rd edition. Sydney: Angus and Robertson.

Enfield, N. J. 2007. *A grammar of Lao.* Berlin: Mouton de Gruyter.

Evans-Pritchard, E. E. 1940. *The Nuer: A description of the modes of livelihood and political institutions of a Nilotic people.* New York: Oxford University Press.

Ferguson, Charles A. 1959. 'Diglossia', *Word* 13: 325–40.

Fortescue, Michael. 1984. *West Greenlandic.* London: Croom Helm.

Frajzyngier, Zygmunt. 1993. *A grammar of Mupun.* Berlin: Dietrich Reimer.

Giridhar, P. P. 1980. *Angami grammar.* Mysore: Central Institute of Indian Languages.

Graczyk, Randolph. 2007. *A grammar of Crow: Apsáalooke Aliláau.* Lincoln, Nebr.: University of Nebraska Press.

Guillaume, Antoine. 2008. *A grammar of Cavineña.* Berlin: Mouton de Gruyter.

Guillaume, Antoine and Rose, Françoise. 2010. 'Sociative causative markers in South American languages: A possible areal feature', pp. 383–402 of *Essais de typologie et de linguistique générale: Mélanges offerts à Denis Creissels,* edited by Franck Floricic. Lyons: ENS editions.

Haas, Mary. 1942. 'The use of numeral classifiers in Thai', *Language* 18: 201–5.

Haiman, John. 1980. *Hua: A Papuan language of the Eastern Highlands of New Guinea.* Amsterdam: John Benjamins.

Hale, Austin and Shrestha, Kedar P. 2006. *Newār (Nepāl Bhāṣā).* Munich: Lincom Europa.

Halpern, A. M. 1942. 'Yuma kinship terms', *American Anthropologist* 44: 425–41.

Harrison, Simon J. 1990. *Stealing people's names: History and politics in a Sepik river cosmology.* Cambridge: Cambridge University Press.

Haviland, John. 1979. 'Guugu Yimidhirr', pp. 1–180 of *Handbook of Australian languages,* Vol. 1, edited by R. M. W. Dixon and Barry J. Blake. Canberra: The Australian National University Press and Amsterdam: John Benjamins.

Iwasaki, Shoichi and Ingkaphirom, Preeya. 2005. *A reference grammar of Thai.* Cambridge: Cambridge University Press.

Jacobsen, William H., Jr. 1964. 'A grammar of the Washo language.' Ph.D. dissertation, University of California at Berkeley.

Jakobson, Roman. 1971. 'Boas's view of grammatical meaning', pp. 489–96 of *Roman Jakobson: Selected writings,* Vol. 2, *Word and language.* The Hague: Mouton.

Jarkey, Nerida. 2006. 'Complement clause types and complementation strategy in White Hmong', pp. 115–36 of *Complementation: A cross-linguistic typology,* edited by R. M. W. Dixon and Alexandra Y. Aikhenvald. Oxford: Oxford University Press.

Jespersen, Otto. 1922. *Language: Its nature, development and origin.* London: George Allen and Unwin.

Jeyapaul, V. Y. 1987. *Karbi grammar.* Mysore: Central Institute for Indian Languages.

Johnson, Samuel. 1755. *A dictionary of the English language...* London: J. and P. Knapton, T. and T. Longman, C. Hitch and L. Hawes, A. Millar, and R. and J. Dodsley.

Kachru, Yamuna. 1976. 'On the semantics of the causative construction in Hindi-Urdu', pp. 353–69 of *Syntax and semantics,* Vol. 6,

The grammar of causative constructions, edited by Masayoshi Shibatani. New York: Academic Press.

Kenesei, István, Vago, Robert M., and Fenyvesi, Anna. 1998. *Hungarian.* London: Routledge.

Kirton, Jean N. 1971. 'Complexities of Yanyula nouns: Interrelationship of linguistics and anthropology', pp. 15–70 of *Papers in Australian Linguistics,* No. 5. Canberra: Pacific Linguistics.

Kwee, John B. 1965. *Teach yourself Indonesian.* London: The English Universities Press.

Li, Charles N. and Thompson, Sandra A. 1981. *Mandarin Chinese: A functional reference grammar.* Berkeley and Los Angeles: University of California Press.

Loogman, Alfons. 1965. *Swahili grammar and syntax.* Louvain: Éditions E. Nauwelaerts.

McWhorter, John H. 2001. 'The world's simplest grammars are creole grammars', *Linguistic Typology* 5: 125–66.

Mahapatra, B. P. 1979. *Malto: An ethnosemantic study.* Mysore: Central Institute of Indian Languages.

Matthews, Stephen and Yip, Virginia. 1994. *Cantonese: A comprehensive grammar.* London: Routledge.

Meggitt, M. J. 1962. *Desert people: A study of the Walbiri Aborigines of Central Australia.* Sydney: Angus and Robertson.

Meillet, Antoine. 1970. *General characteristics of the Germanic languages,* translated by William P. Dismules. Coral Gables, Fla.: University of Miami Press. [Original French edition in 1917.]

Mithun, Marianne. 1999. *The languages of native North America.* Cambridge: Cambridge University Press

Noonan, Michael. 1992. *A grammar of Lango.* Berlin: Mouton de Gruyter.

Ogden, C. K. 1932. *The A B C of Basic English.* (In Basic). London: Kegan Paul, Trench, Trubner.

Osborn, Henry A., Jr. 1967. 'Warao III: Verbs and suffixes', *International Journal of American Linguistics* 33: 46–64.

Payne, Doris L. 1980. 'Switch-reference in Chickasaw', pp. 89–118 of *Studies of switch-reference,* edited by Pamela Munro. UCLA Papers in Syntax, Vol. 8. Los Angeles: Department of Linguistics, UCLA.

Payne. Doris L. 2003. 'Maa color terms and their use as human descriptors', *Anthropological Linguistics* 45: 169–200.

Quirk, Randolph and Wrenn, C. L. 1957. *An Old English grammar.* 2nd edition. London: Methuen.

Roberts, John R. 1987. *Amele.* London: Croom Helm.

Sadock, Jerrold M. 1984. 'West Greenlandic', pp. 189–214 of *Interrogativity: A colloquium on the grammar, typology and pragmatics of questions in seven diverse languages,* edited by William S. Chisholm. Amsterdam: John Benjamins.

Saeed, John I. 1993. *Somali reference grammar.* 2nd revised edition. Kensington, Md.: Dunwoody Press.

Saksena, Anuradha. 1982. 'Contact in causation', *Language* 58: 820–31.

Sampson, Geoffrey, Gil, David, and Trudgill, Peter. 2009. Editors of *Language complexity as an evolving variable.* Oxford: Oxford University Press.

Schachter, Paul and Otanes, Fe T. 1972. *Tagalog reference grammar.* Berkeley and Los Angeles: University of California Press.

Shibatani, Masayoshi. 1990. *The languages of Japan.* Cambridge: Cambridge University Press.

Sinclair, John. 2001. Founder editor-in-chief of *Collins Cobuild English dictionary for advanced learners.* Glasgow: HarperCollins.

Smith, Ian and Johnson, Steve. 2000. 'Kugu Nganhcara', pp. 357–489 of *The handbook of Australian languages,* Vol. 5, edited by R. M. W. Dixon and Barry J. Blake. Melbourne: Oxford University Press.

Sneddon, James N. 1996. *Indonesian reference grammar.* Sydney: Allen and Unwin.

Suhandano. 2015. *Grammatical relations in Javanese: A short description.* Munich: Lincom Europa.

Svantesson, Jan-Olof. 1983. *Kammu phonology and morphology*. Travaux de l'institut de linguistique de Lund, No. 18.

Tonoike, Shigeo. 1978. 'On the causative constructions in Japanese', pp. 3–29 of *Problems in Japanese syntax and semantics*, edited by J. Hinds and I. Howard. Tokyo: Kaitakusha.

Tosco, Mauro. 2001. *The Dhaasanac language: Grammar, texts, vocabulary of a Cushitic language of Ethiopia*. Cologne: Rüdiger Köppe.

Trudgill, Peter. 2011. *Sociolinguistic typology: Social determinants of linguistic complexity*. Oxford: Oxford University Press.

Tsujimura, Natsuko. 1996. *An introduction to Japanese linguistics*. Oxford: Blackwell.

Waag, Christine. 2010. *The Fur verb and its context*. Cologne: Rüdiger Köppe.

Walsh, Michael J. 2012. *The Muriny[a]pata language of north-west Australia*. Munich: Lincom Europa.

Watkins, Calvert. 1985. *The American Heritage dictionary of Indo-European roots*. Boston: Houghton Mifflin.

Wells, J. C. 1982. *Accents of English*, Vol. 1, *An introduction*. Cambridge: Cambridge University Press.

Index

Index

Index

phonemes 28–32, 202
phonology 23–31, 222–5
phrasal verbs 17, 171–2
Pirahã 145–6, 251
pivots 71–3, 96–100, 104, 232–3
Plato 10, 248
plural *see* number in grammar
polar questions 6, 48–53, 55, 63,
    113, 163, 175
Portuguese 68, 72, 82–4, 93, 109–11,
    115–17, 140, 199, 209, 222, 241
possession 57–60, 174–5, 183–4,
    228–9
    see also inalienable possession
predicate 60
prediction 15–17
primary verbs 34
primitive language 4–7
pronouns 16, 37–41, 177, 225–6
Punjabi 204

Quechua 190, 204
questions 48–53, 227–8
    see also interrogative mood, polar
    questions
Quirk, Randolph 248

racist evaluation 20–1
reciprocals 98–100, 237
redundancy 30, 162, 193, 214
    grammatical 115–18
    phonological 30–1
    semantic 118–21
reduplication 99, 132–7, 220–2
reflexives 97–100, 236–7
relative clause constructions 28,
    69–73, 208, 231
repetition 121–4
Roberts, John R. 249
role of language 2–4
Romance loans 156–7, 165–6
Rose, Françoise 252

Rumanian 16
Russian 16, 52, 76, 82, 88, 198,
    207–8, 224, 241

S (intransitive subject function)
    60–6, 69–73, 80, 95–105
Sadock, Jerrold M. 249
Saeed, John I. 249
Saksena, Anuradha 250
Sampson, Geoffrey 248
Schachter, Paul 250
secondary concepts 34–5
semi-synonyms 13, 123,
    165–7, 188
Shibatani, Masayoshi 250, 252
shifters 35–41, 48
Shrestha, Kedar P. 249
Sinclair, John 252
Slavic langages 9, 88–9, 177–8, 284
Smith, Ian 251
Sneddon, James N. 253
Somali 56, 249
Spanish 57, 68, 72, 76, 198, 202, 222,
    241, 253
specification 149–55
speech acts 48–53
statements 48–53
style 3, 121–4, 131, 164–5, 189
subject function. *see* S (intransitve
    subject) and A (transitive
    subject), of which it is a
    combination
subordination 28, 56, 60–73, 208,
    228, 231–2, 253
Suhandano 250
suppletion 113–15, 251
Svantesson, Jan-Olof 250
Swahili 78–9, 116–17, 138, 176
Swedish 207
switch reference 72–3, 233
syllable structure 29–31, 224
synonymy 163–7

271

Index

BOOKS BY R. M. W. DIXON

BOOKS ON LINGUISTICS
Linguistic Science and Logic
What *is* Language? A New Approach to Linguistic Description
The Dyirbal Language of North Queensland
A Grammar of Yidiɲ
The Languages of Australia
Where Have All the Adjectives Gone? And Other Essays in Semantics
and Syntax
Searching for Aboriginal Languages: Memoirs of a Field Worker
A Grammar of Boumaa Fijian
A New Approach to English Grammar, on Semantic Principles
Words of Our Country: Stories, Place Names and Vocabulary in Yidiny
Ergativity
The Rise and Fall of Languages
Australian Languages: Their Nature and Development
The Jarawara Language of Southern Amazonia
A Semantic Approach to English Grammar
Basic Linguistic Theory, Vol. 1, Methodology
Basic Linguistic Theory, Vol. 2, Grammatical Topics
Basic Linguistic Theory, Vol. 3, Further Grammatical Topics
I am a Linguist
Making New Words: Morphological Derivation in English
Edible Gender, Mother-in-law Style and Other Grammatical Wonders:
Studies in Dyirbal, Yidiñ and Warrgamay

with Alexandra Y. Aikhenvald
Language at Large: Essays on Syntax and Semantics

with Grace Koch
Dyirbal Song Poetry: The Oral Literature of an Australian Rainforest People

with Bruce Moore, W. S. Ramson and Mandy Thomas
Australian Aboriginal Words in English: Their Origin and Meaning

BOOKS ON MUSIC
with John Godrich
Recording the Blues

with John Godrich and Howard Rye
Blues and Gospel Records, 1890–1943

NOVELS *(under the name Hosanna Brown)*
I Spy, You Die
Death upon a Spear

EDITOR OF BOOKS ON LINGUISTICS
Grammatical Categories in Australian Languages
Studies in Ergativity

with Barry J. Blake
Handbook of Australian Languages, Vols 1–5

with Martin Duwell
The Honey Ant Men's Love Song, and Other Aboriginal Song Poems
Little Eva at Moonlight Creek: Further Aboriginal Song Poems

with Alexandra Y. Aikhenvald
The Amazonian Languages
Changing Valency: Case studies in Transitivity
Areal Diffusion and Genetic Inheritance: Problems in Comparative
Linguistics
Word: A Cross-linguistic Typology
Studies in Evidentiality
Adjective Classes: A Cross-linguistic Typology
Serial Verb Constructions: A Cross-linguistic Typology
Complementation: A Cross-linguistic Typology
Grammars in Contact: A Cross-linguistic Typology
The Semantics of Clause-linking: A Cross-linguistic Typology
Possession and Ownership: A Cross-linguistic Typology
The Grammar of Knowledge: A Cross-linguistic Typology
The Cambridge Handbook of Linguistic Typology

with Alexandra Y. Aikhenvald and Masayuki Onishi
Non-canonical Marking of Subjects and Objects

Printed and bound by CPI Group (UK) Ltd, Croydon, CR0 4YY